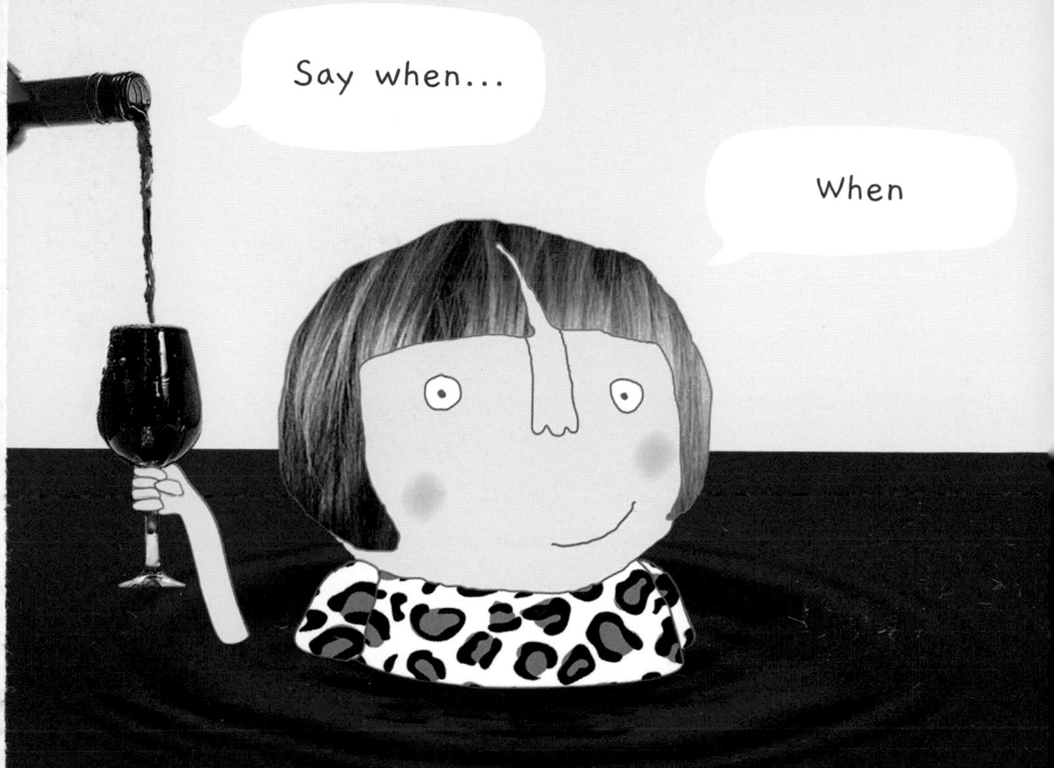
Say when...
When

Wine not?

A book of grown-up decisions

HarperCollinsPublishers
1 London Bridge Street
London SE1 9GF

www.harpercollins.co.uk

HarperCollinsPublishers
Macken House, 39/40 Mayor Street Upper,
Dublin 1, D01 C9W8, Ireland

First published by HarperCollinsPublishers 2022

3 5 7 9 10 8 6 4 2

A catalogue record of this book is
available from the British Library

ISBN 978-0-00-853128-7

Printed and bound in Latvia

FSC
www.fsc.org
MIX
Paper from
responsible sources
FSC™ C007454

This book is produced from
independently certified FSC™ paper to
ensure responsible forest management.

For more information visit:
www.harpercollins.co.uk/green

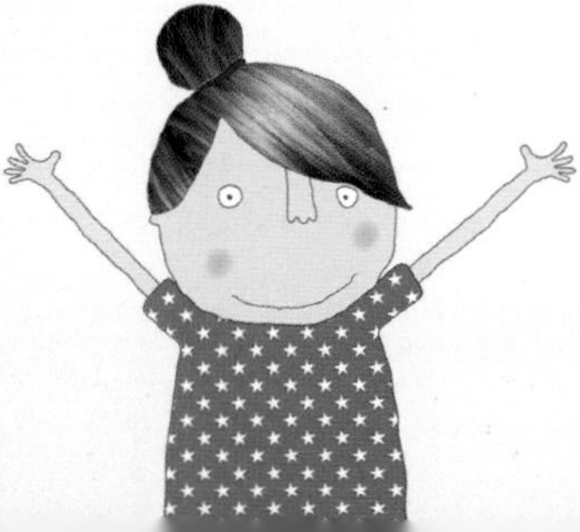

Contents

For my gang,
Tim, George, Rory and Lily,
without whom I might have become a doctor or
something and never got involved in this silliness.

Intro

Hello, I'm Rosie.
The Rosie who Makes The Thing.

Welcome to my little book of nonsense, inspired
by people like you and me and the everyday
ridiculousness of modern life.

For those who eat cake for breakfast, those who are
born to be wild (until about 9pm) and those who
pour BIG wines – this is for you.

I hope it makes you smile...and gives you something
to read on the loo instead of looking at your phone.

Rosie x

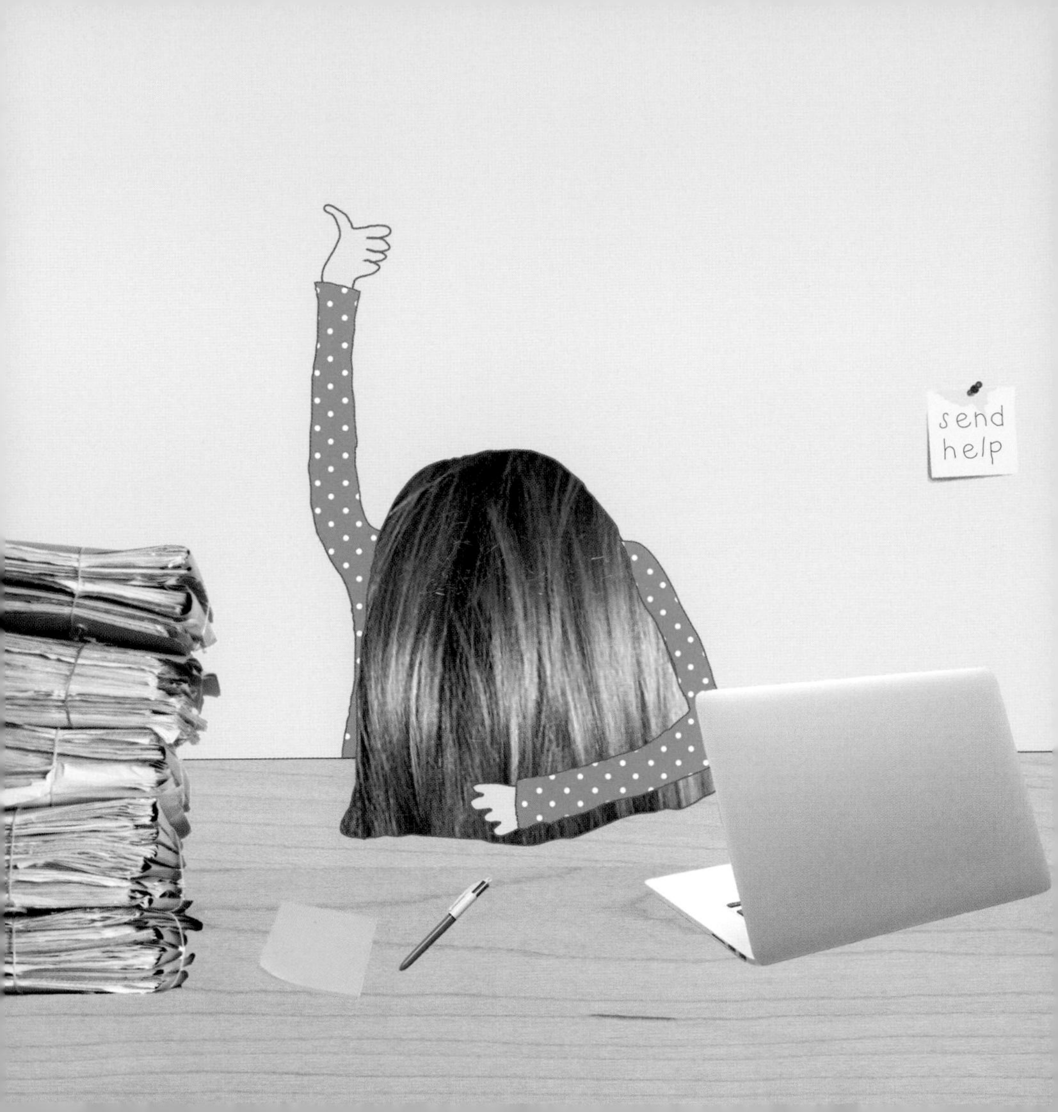
send
help

Working 9-5

stuff

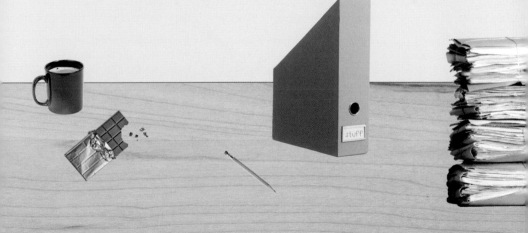

Loading...

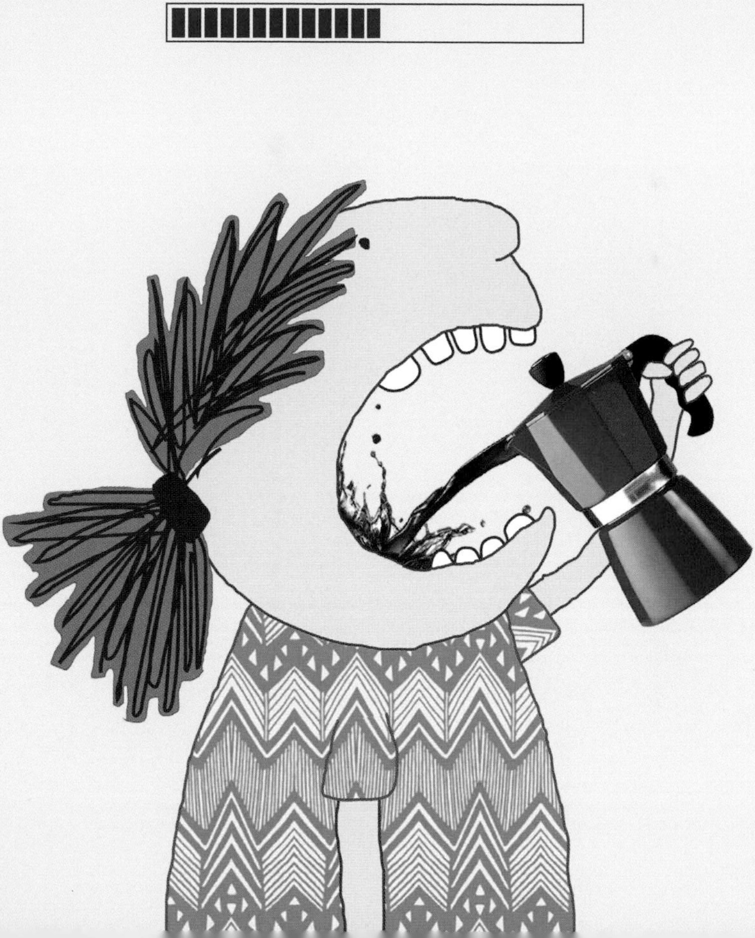

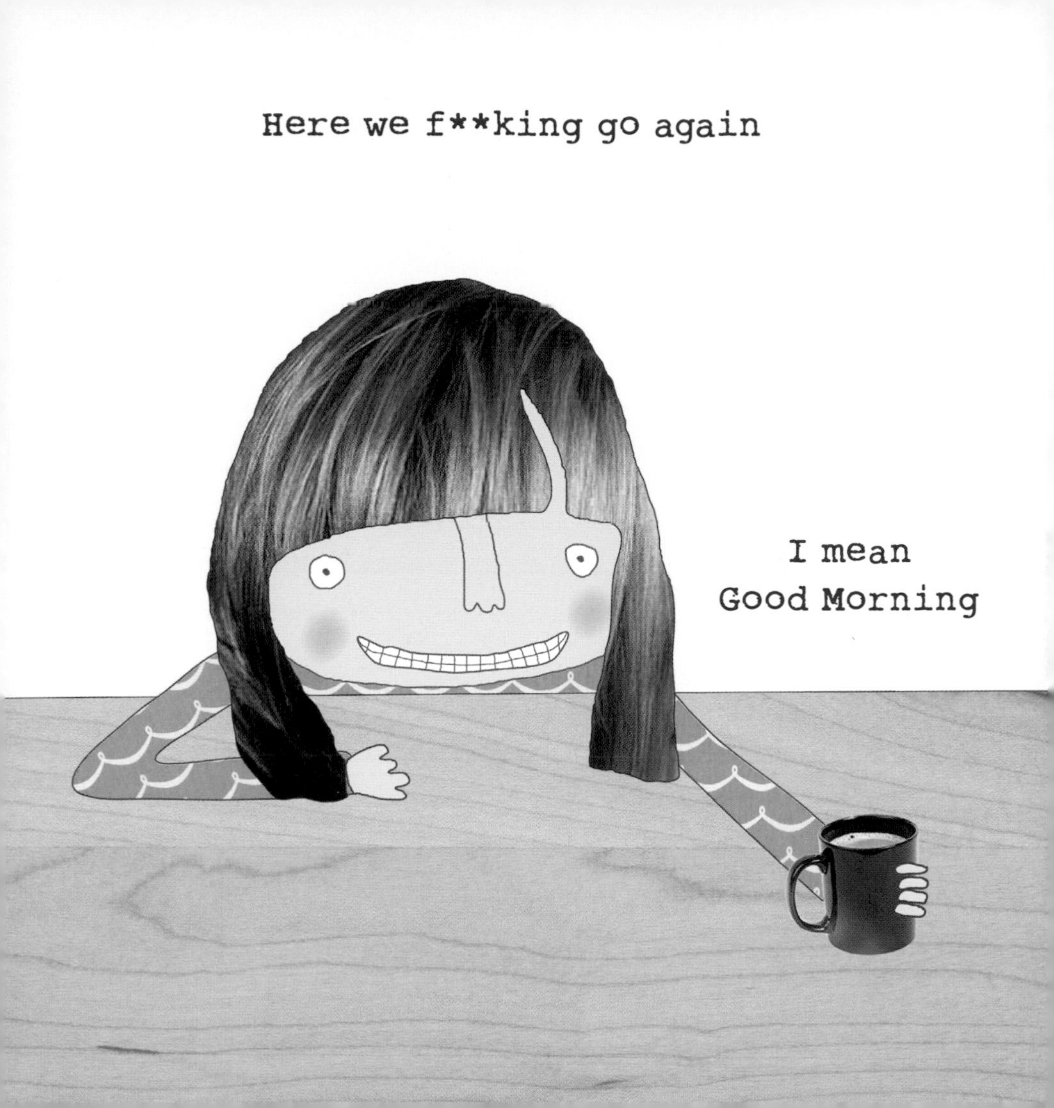
Here we f**king go again
I mean
Good Morning

Every office has 3 people
who do all the work

...and 15 people who
just walk around with
salads

Refreshed and ready for
another week of this bullshit

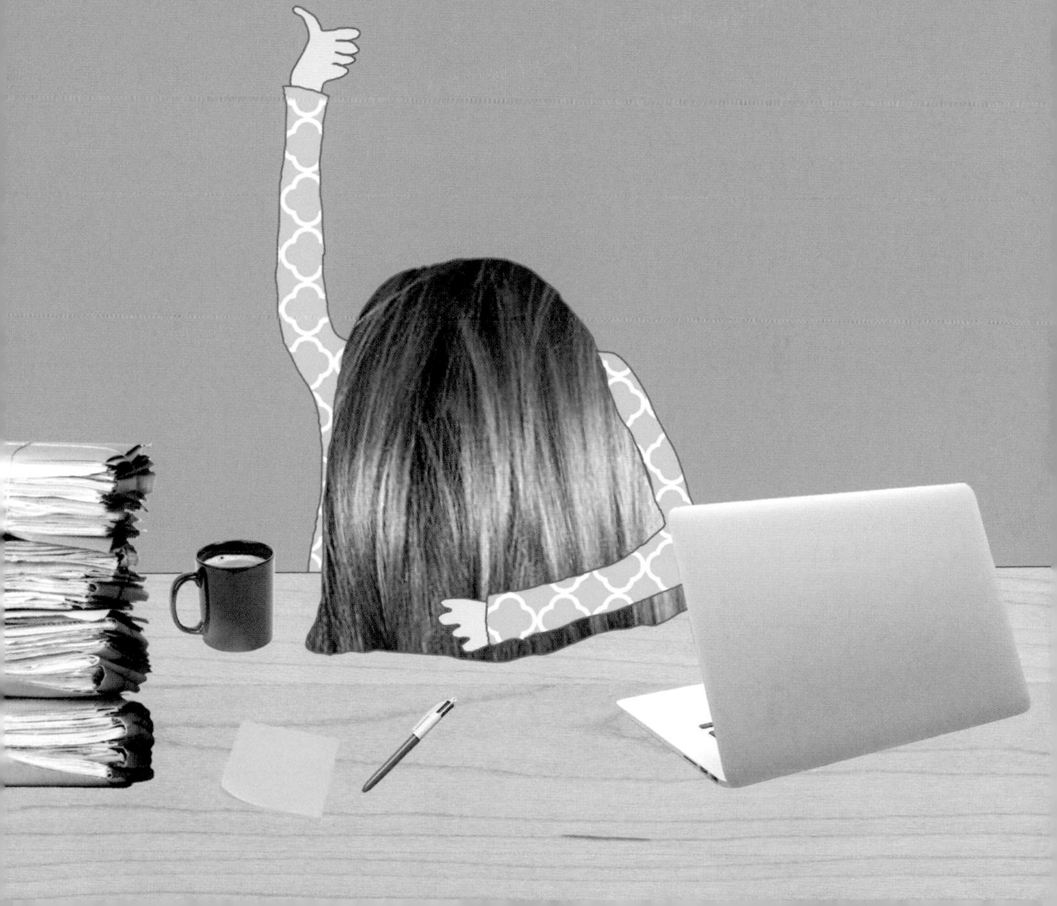

There just aren't enough hours in the day

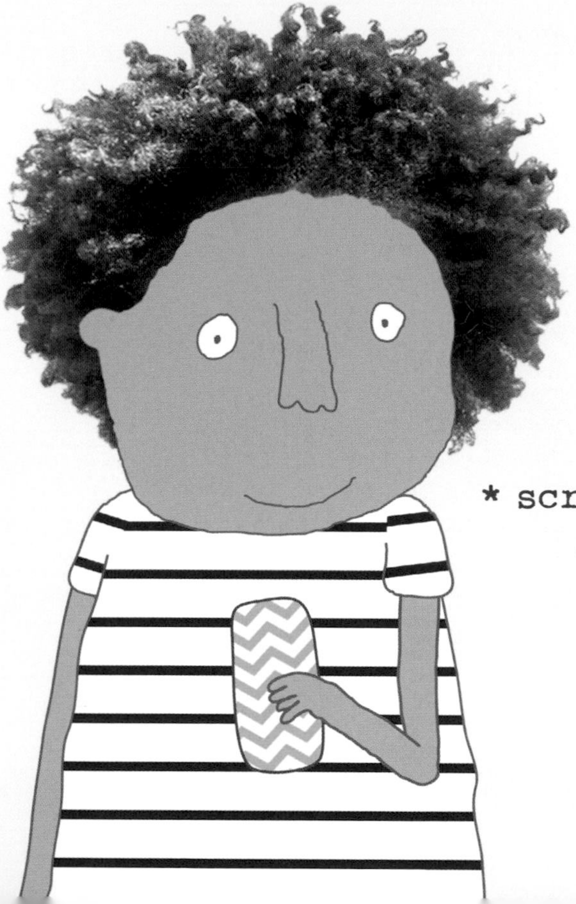

* screen time 11 hours
and 46 mins *

I'm a strong, independent woman

But I'm already wrapped up in this blanket
so if you could get me a snack and a coffee
that would be great

TGIB
Thank God It's Bedtime

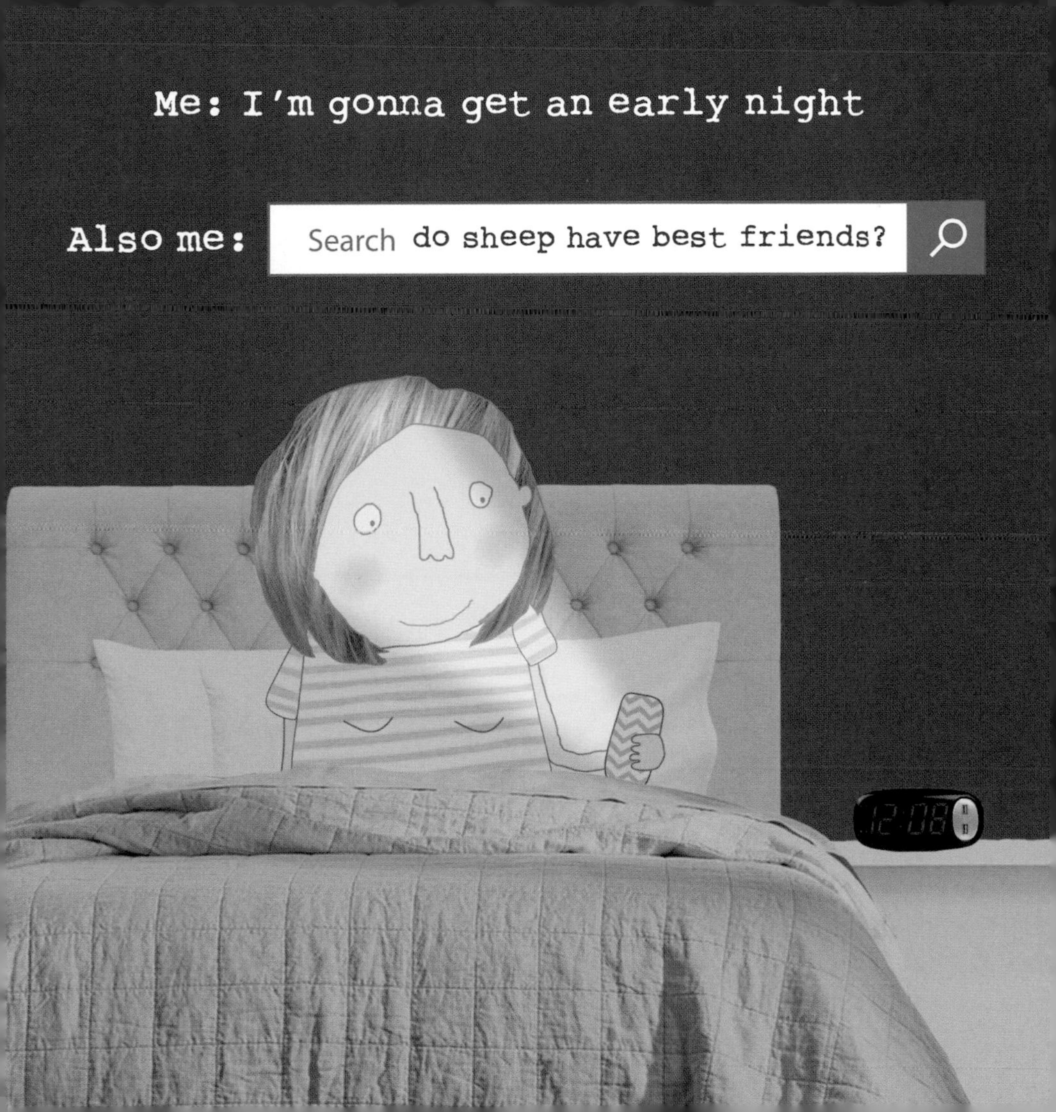
Me: I'm gonna get an early night
Also me:
Search do sheep have best friends?
12:08

Here comes the weekend!
Let's party! Let's...

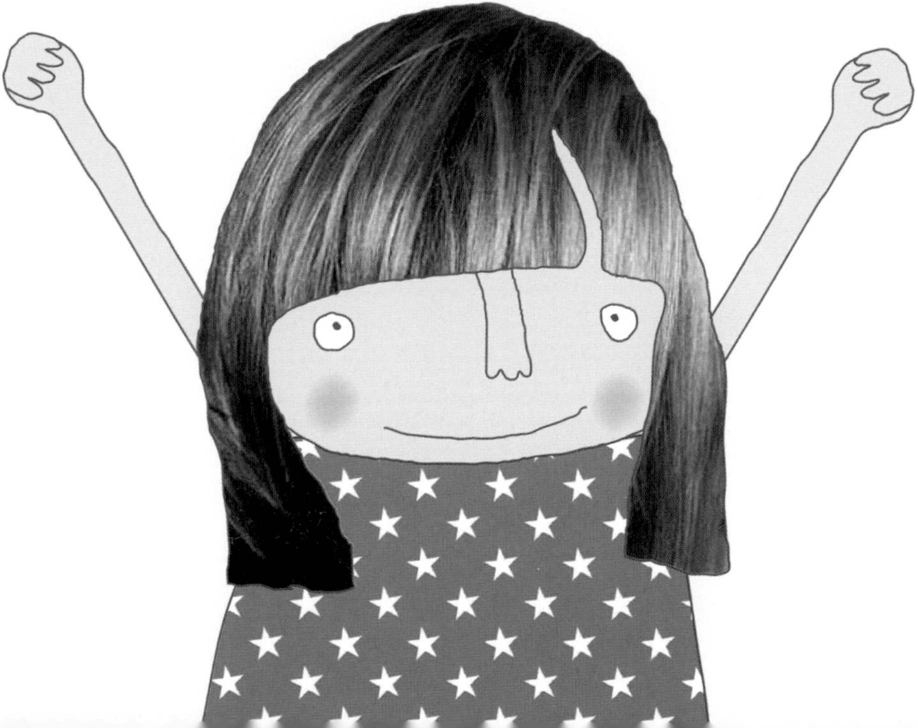

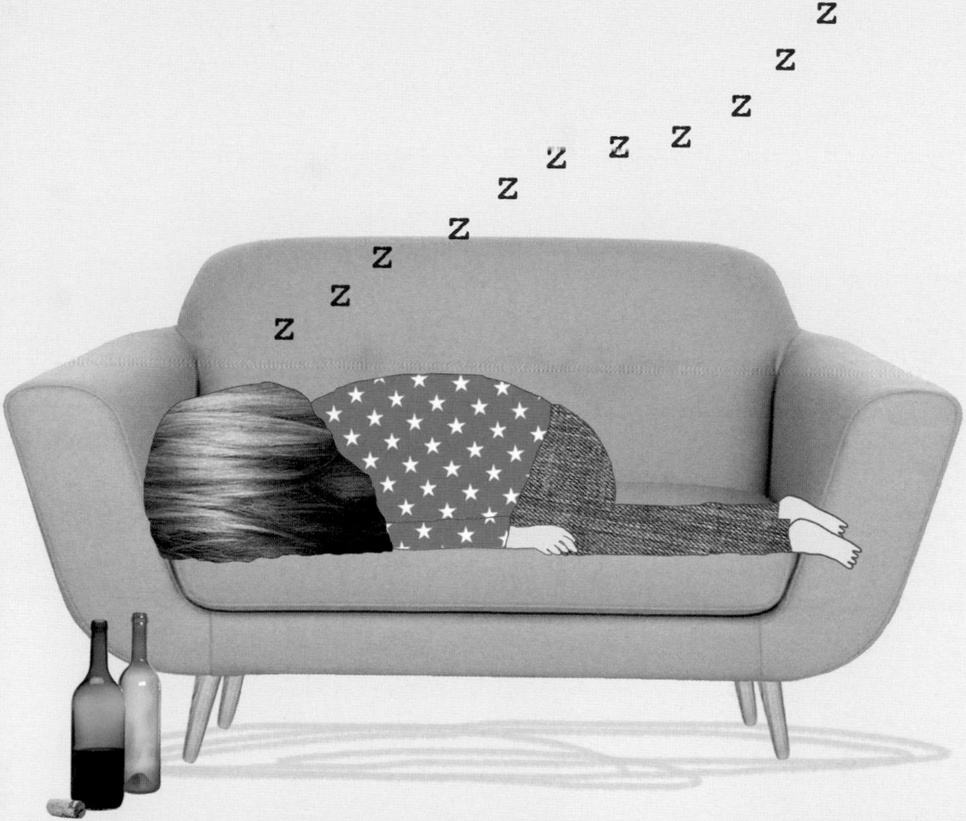
Z Z Z Z Z Z Z Z Z Z Z

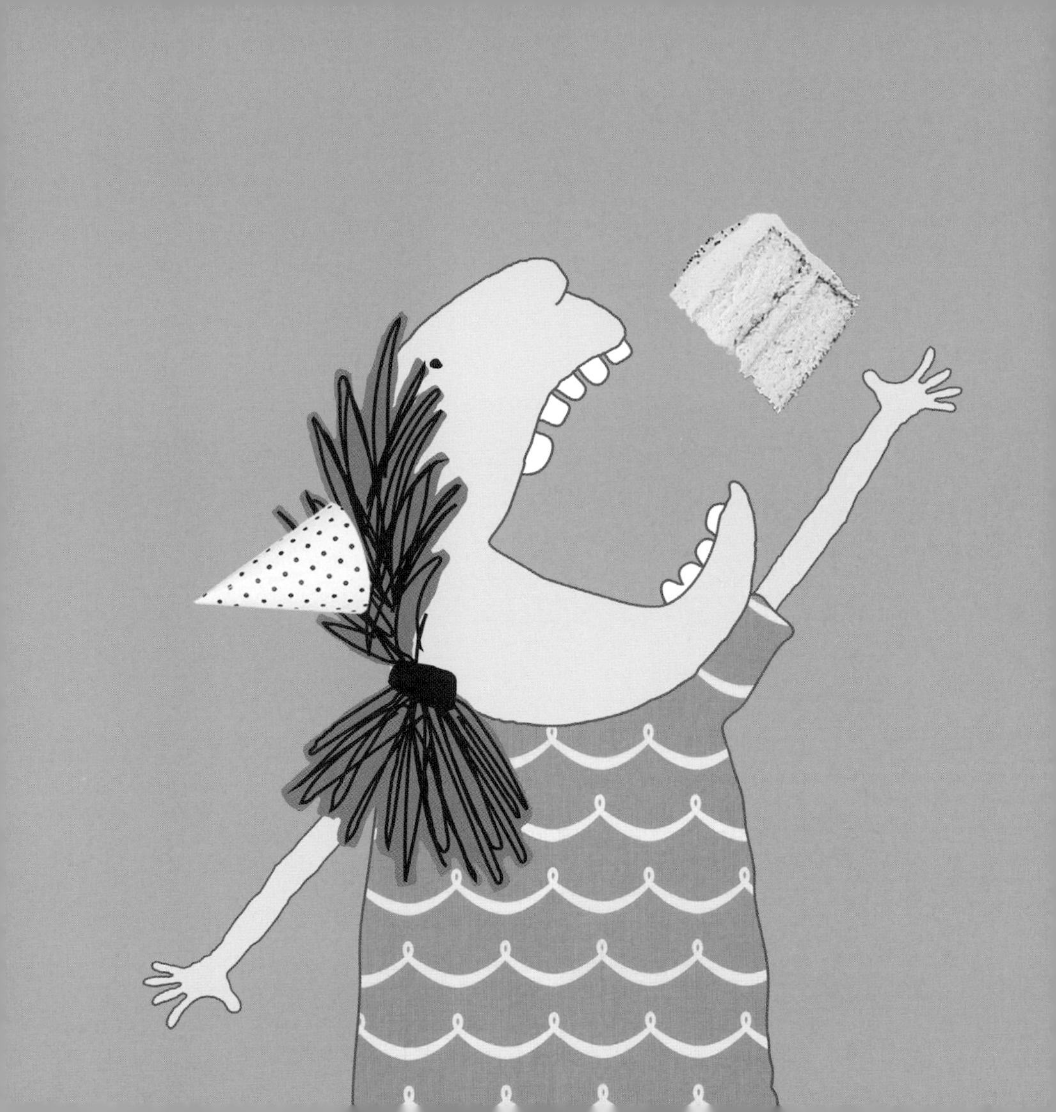

Cakey-ness

Don't rely on a man to make you happy

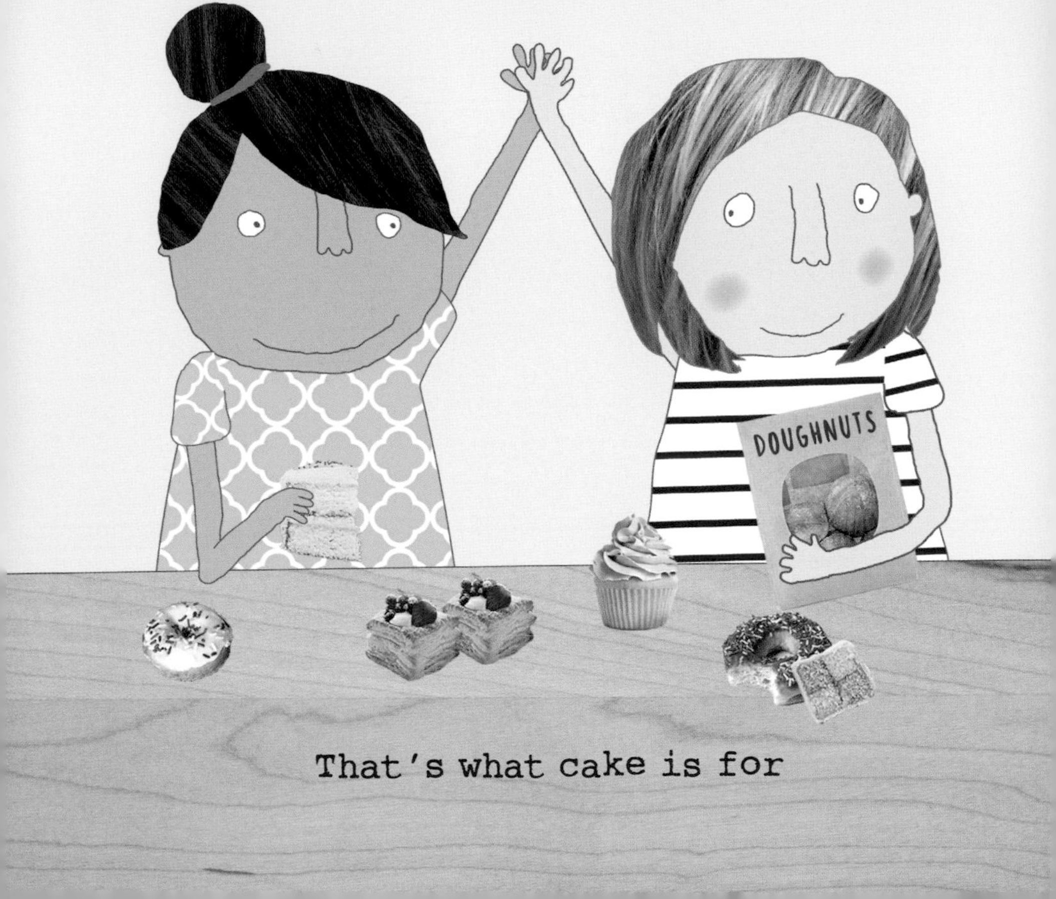
DOUGHNUTS

That's what cake is for

You know when you buy a bag of salad
and it gets all brown and soggy?

Biscuits
don't do that

Bikini season is just around the corner

Unfortunately so is the Chinese takeaway

Cake
Because no great party ever
started with a salad

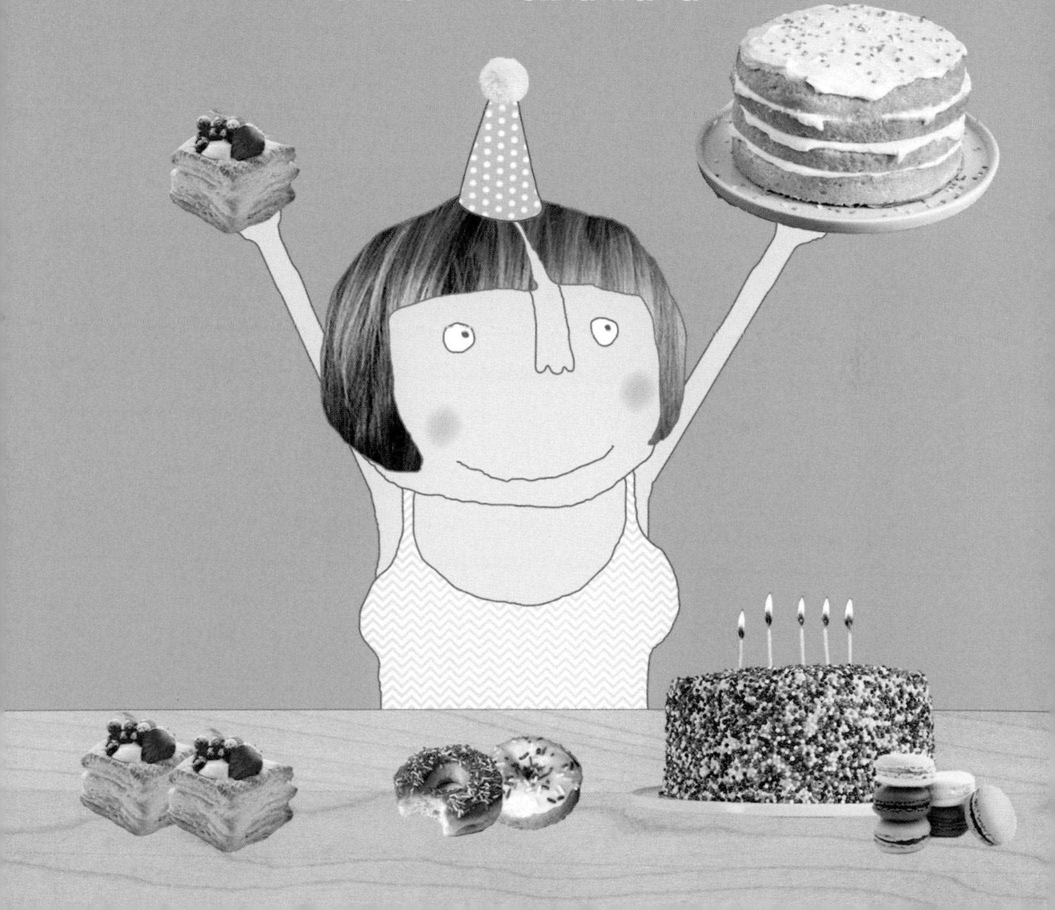

Carpe cakem
(Seize the cake)

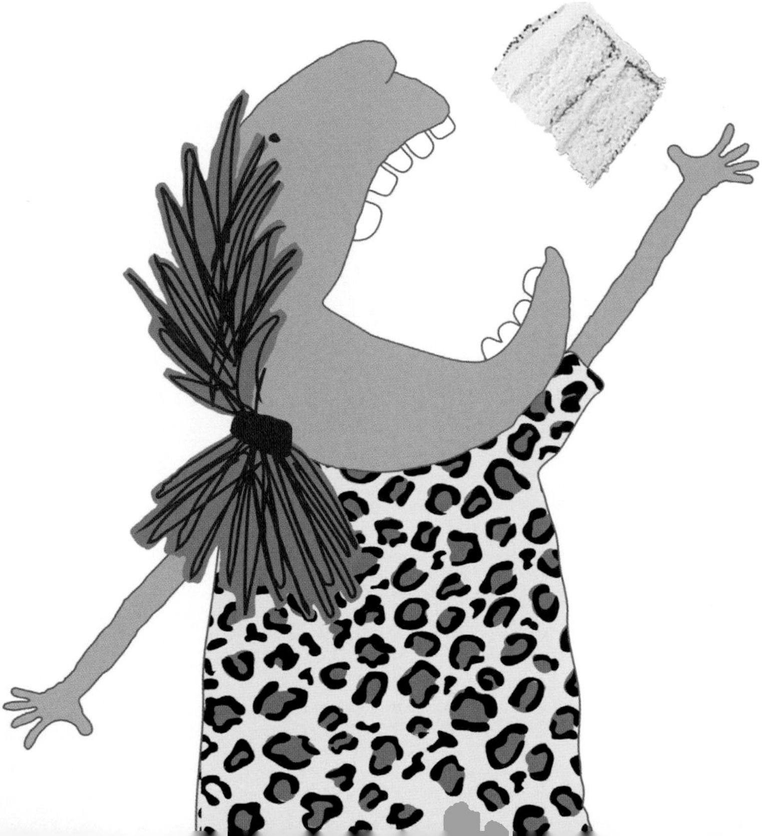

These 5:2 diets are totally manageable

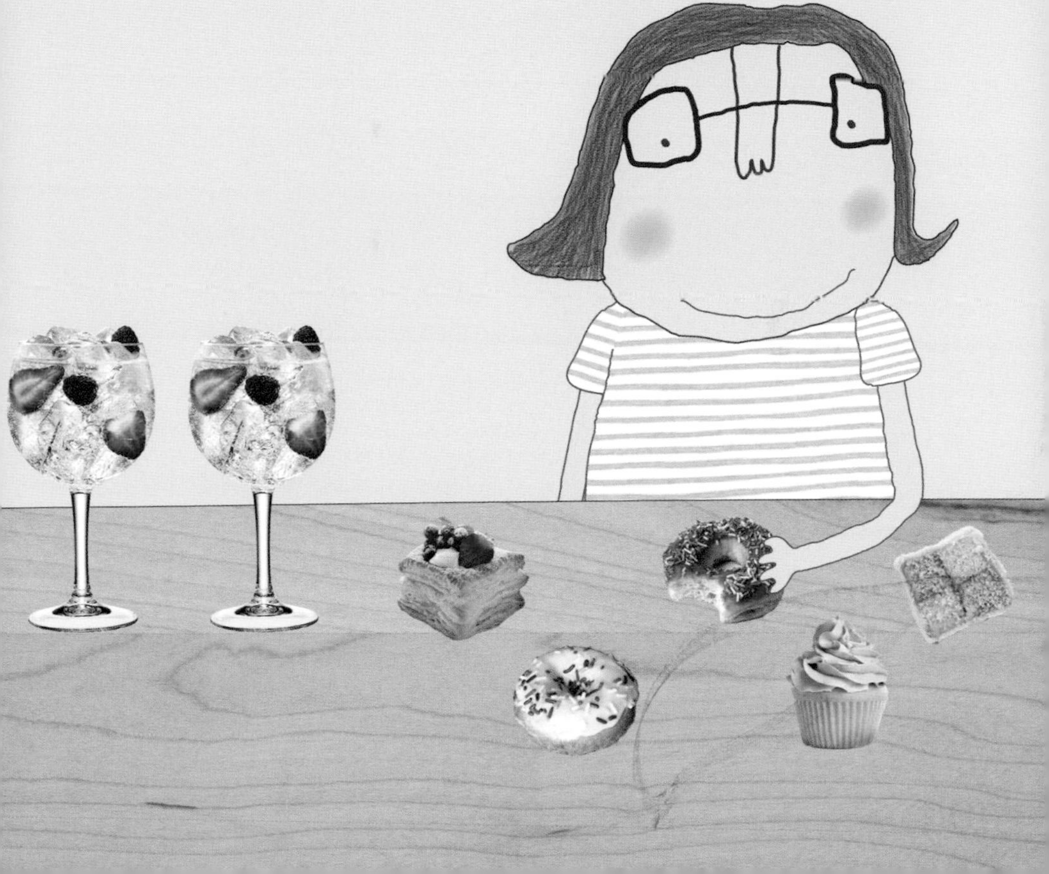

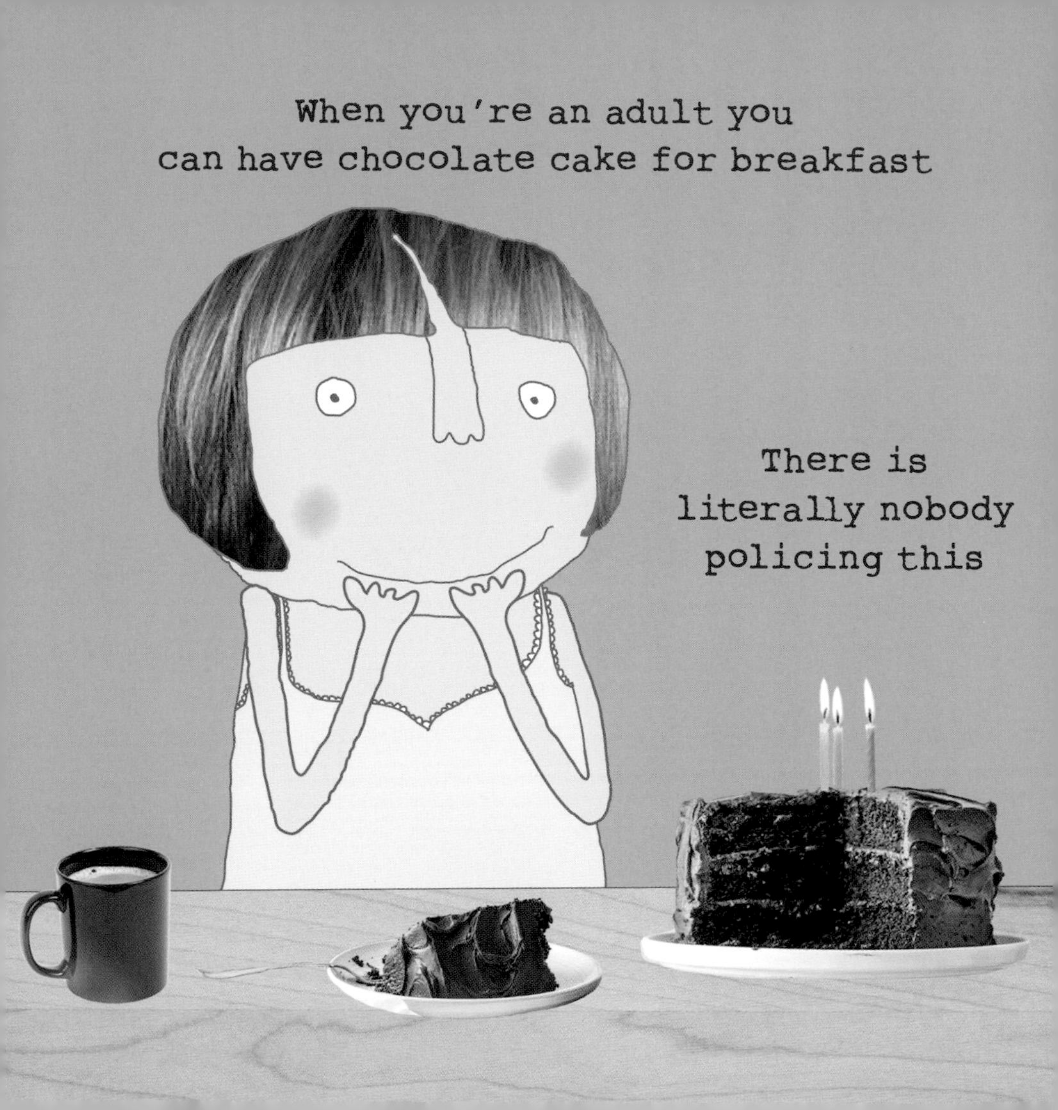
When you're an adult you
can have chocolate cake for breakfast
There is
literally nobody
policing this

Breakfast: 300 kcal

Lunch: 400 kcal

Dinner: 600 kcal

Evening snack: 8,600 kcal

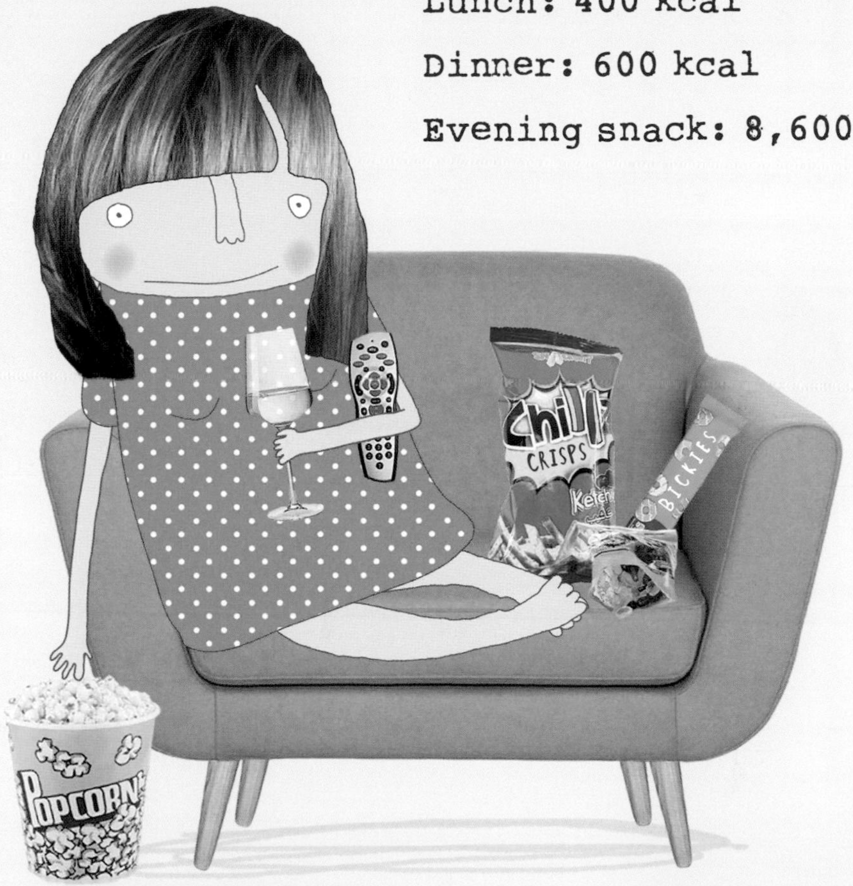
Chilli
CRISPS
BICKIES
POPCORN

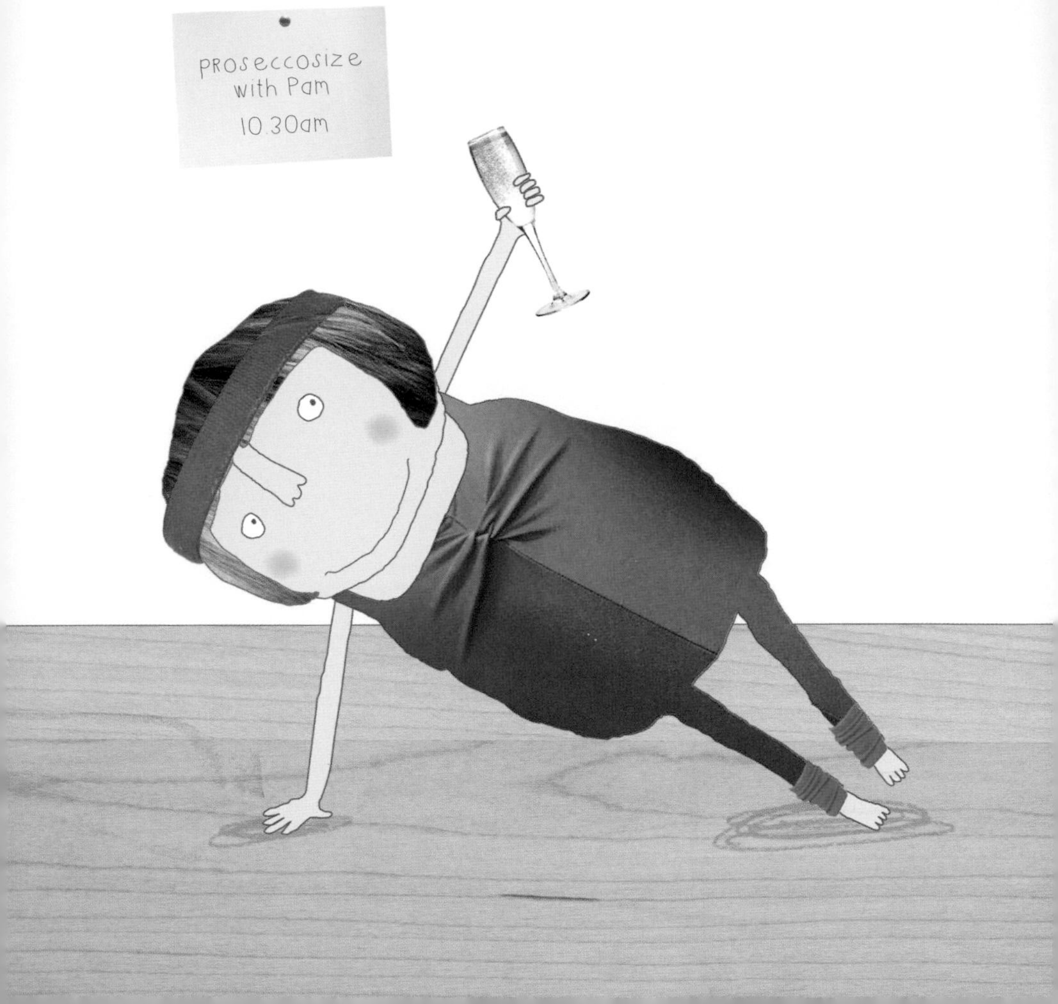
Proseccosize
with Pam
10.30am

Witness the fitness

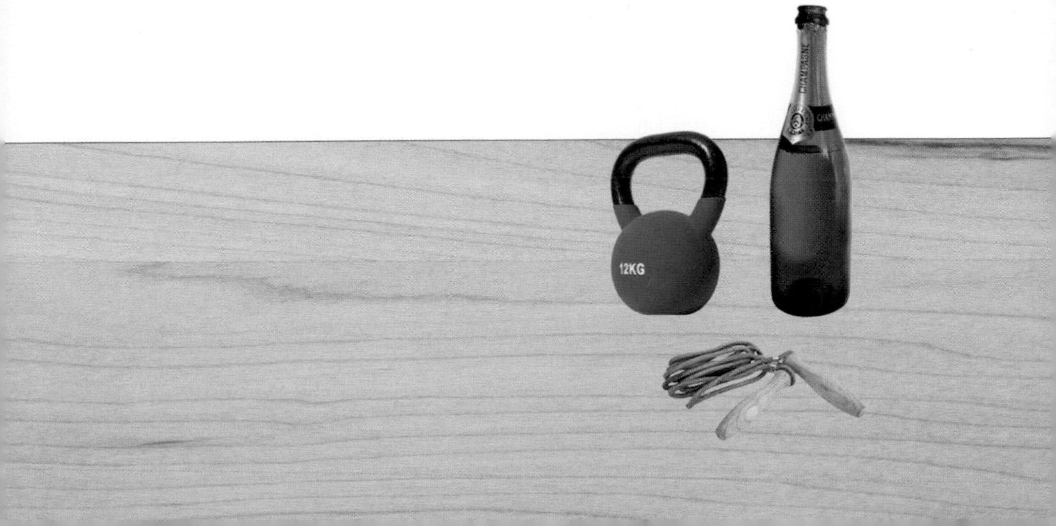
CHAMPAGNE
12KG

That awkward moment
when you're wearing Nikes
and you can't do it

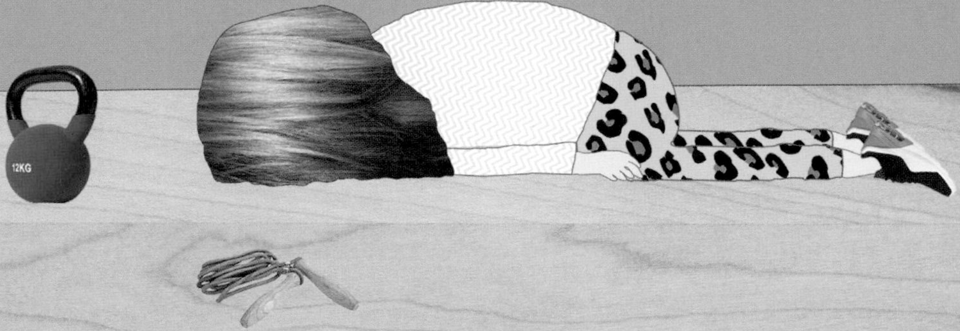
12KG

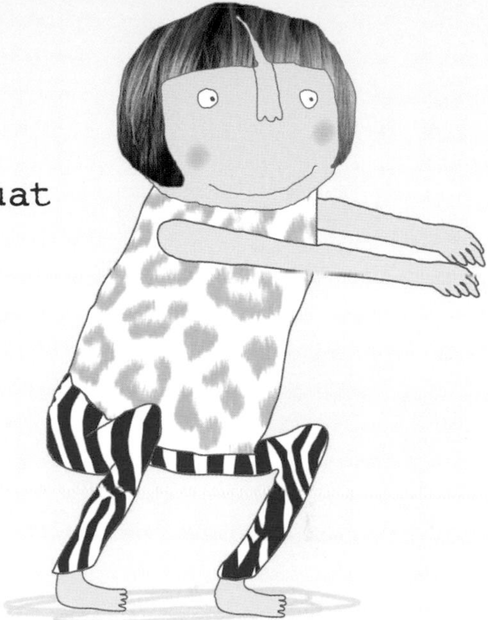

Squat

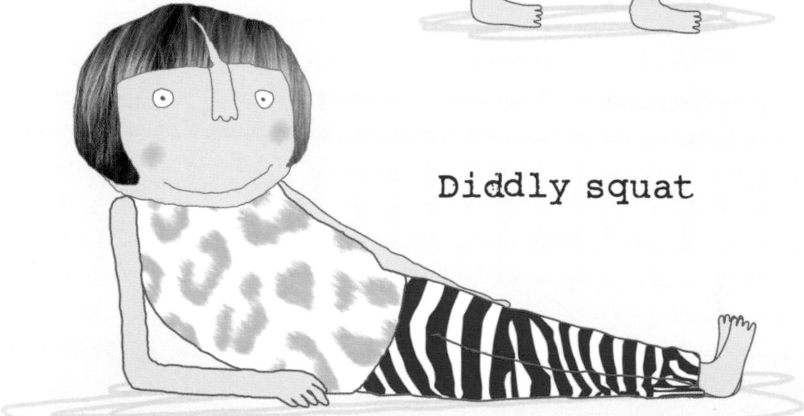

Diddly squat

I do yoga 3 times a week and plan vegan meals a week in advance

I eat cake over the sink so I don't get crumbs in my bed

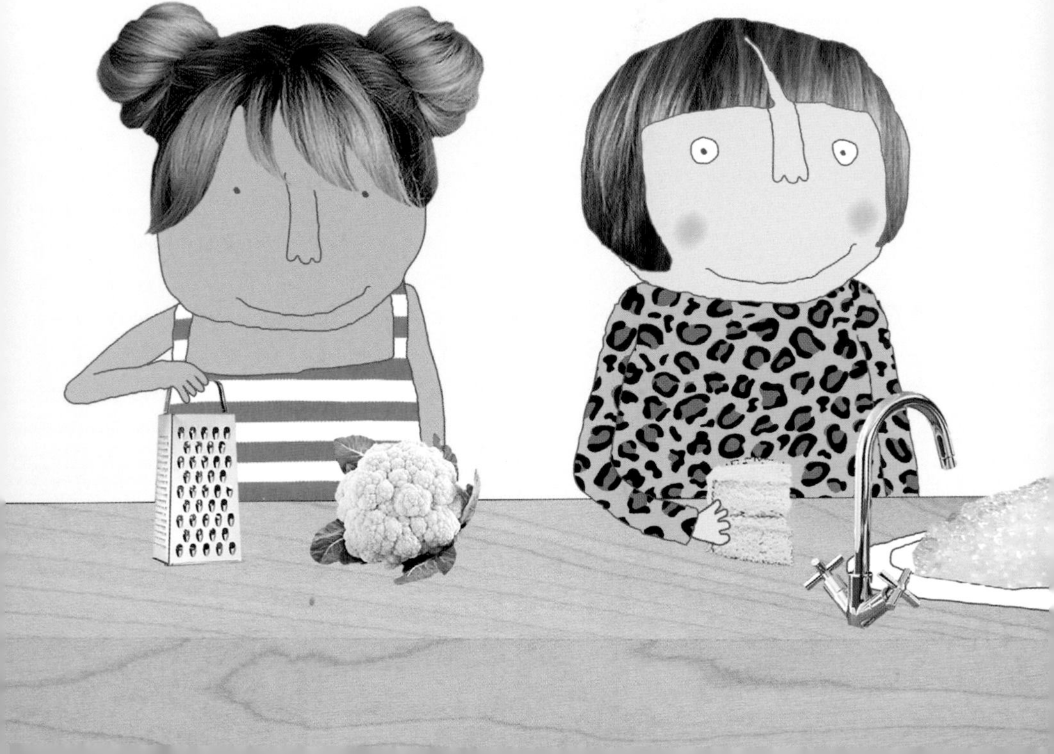

There's a runner inside all of us
screaming to get out

But we can usually shut her up with a biscuit

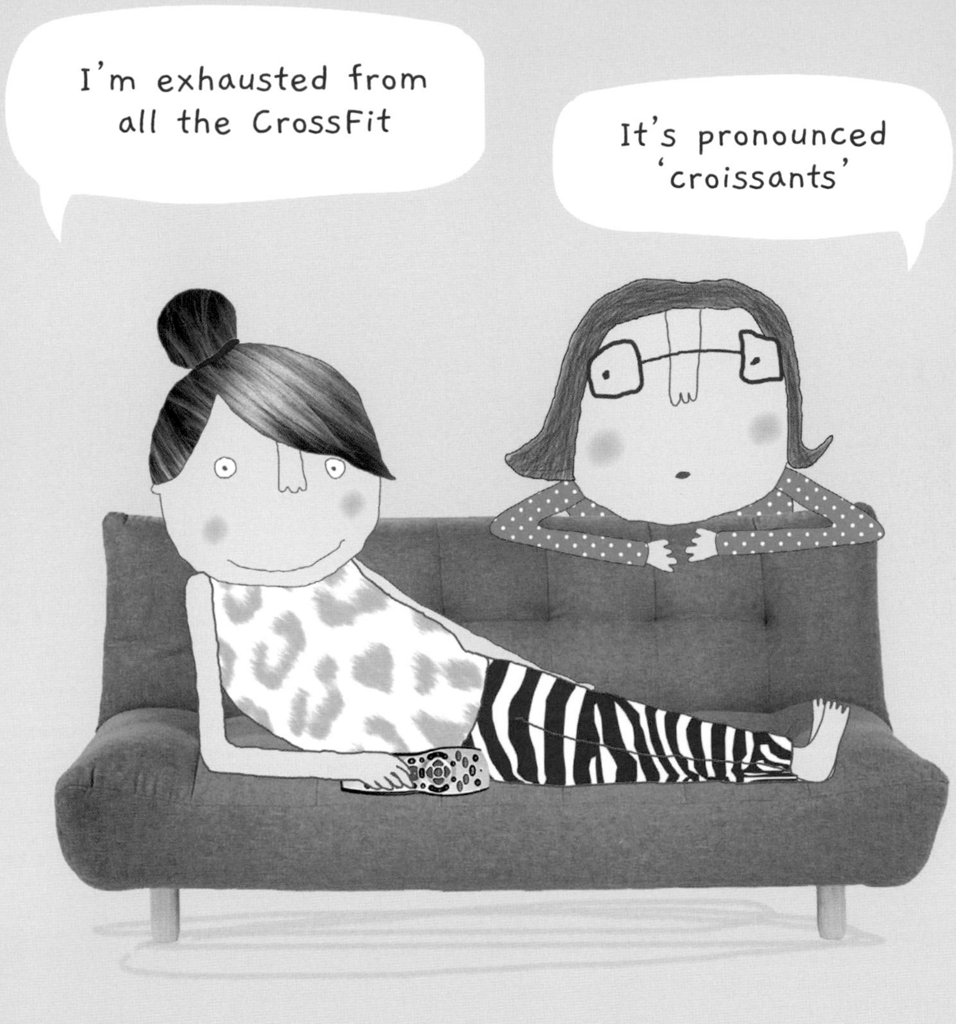
I'm exhausted from all the CrossFit
It's pronounced 'croissants'

Yoga class?
I thought you said
pour a glass!

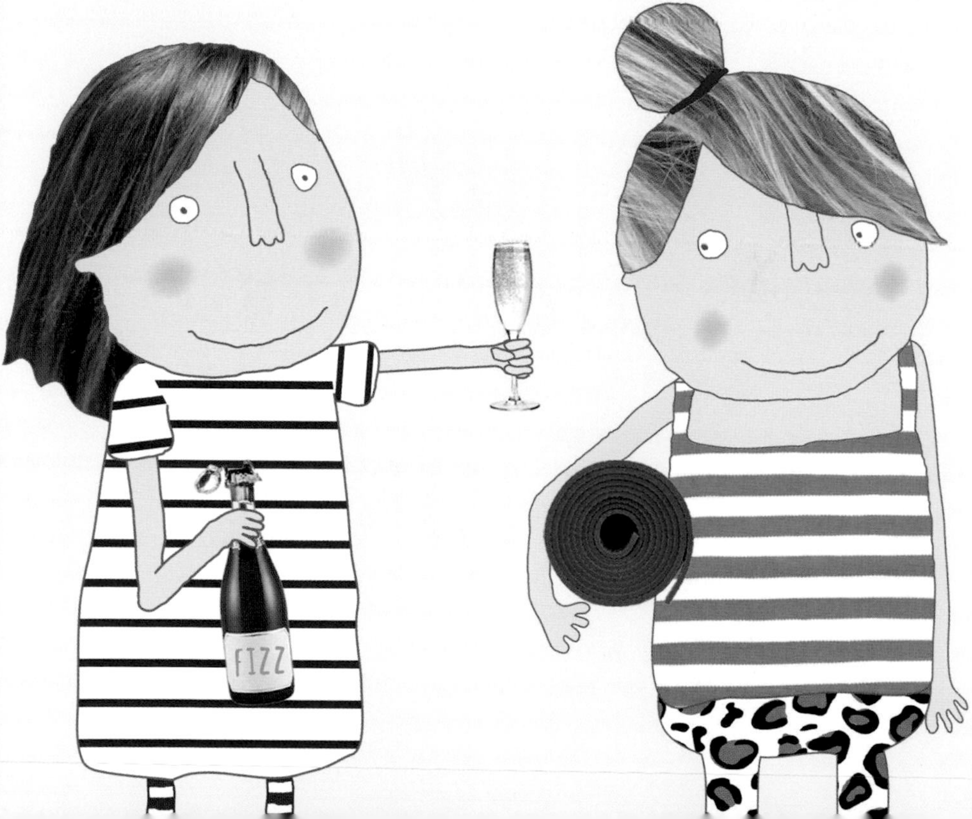
FIZZ

Witness the fitness

Golf

Like real sport but slower and for old people

You've
still got it

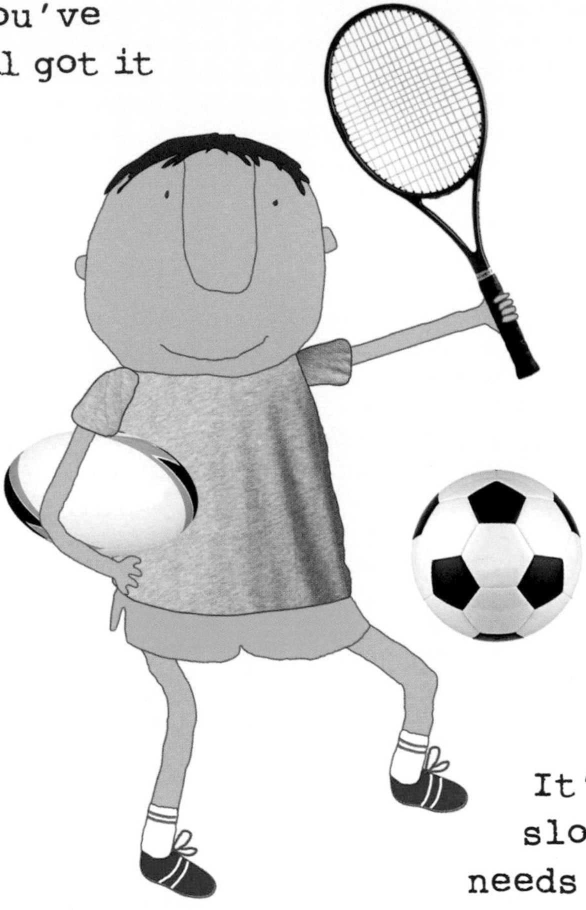

It's just
slower and
needs ibuprofen

I haven't managed to lose any weight so now I'm focusing on getting taller

How to get a beach body

1. Go to the beach

2. Have a body

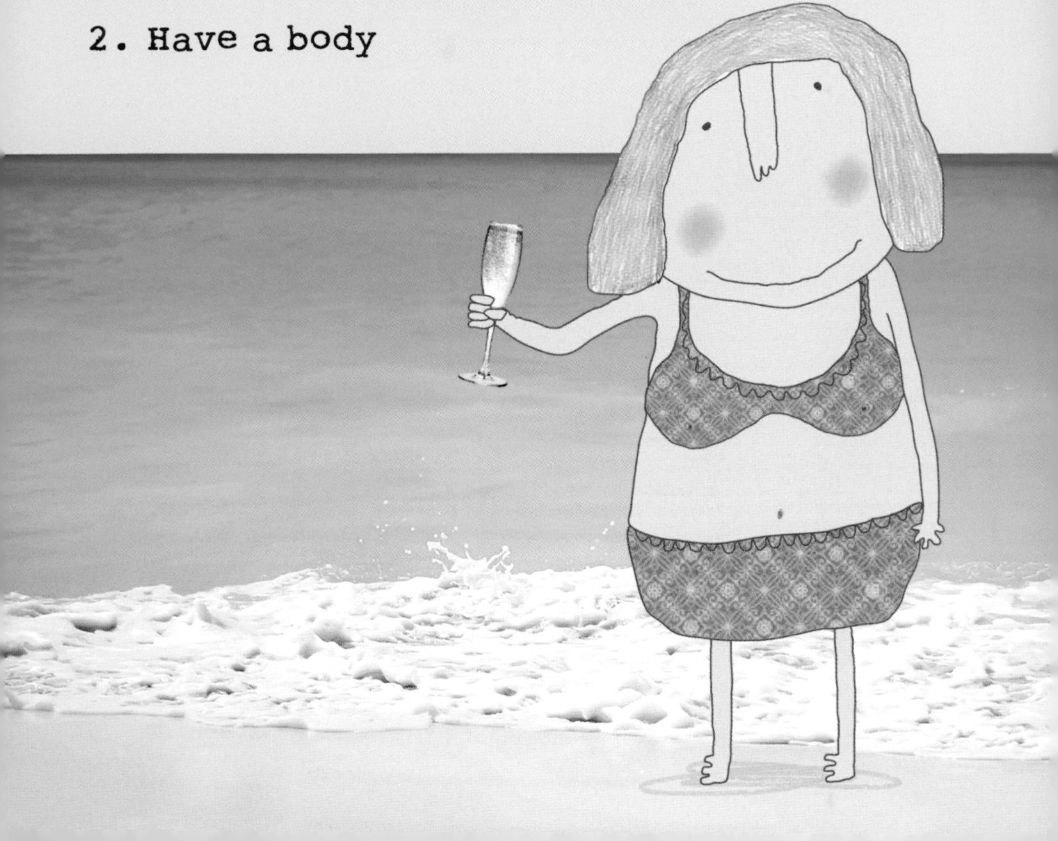

20% cycling
80% cake

I'm afraid if I start working out I'll be too sexy

Betterer than Federer

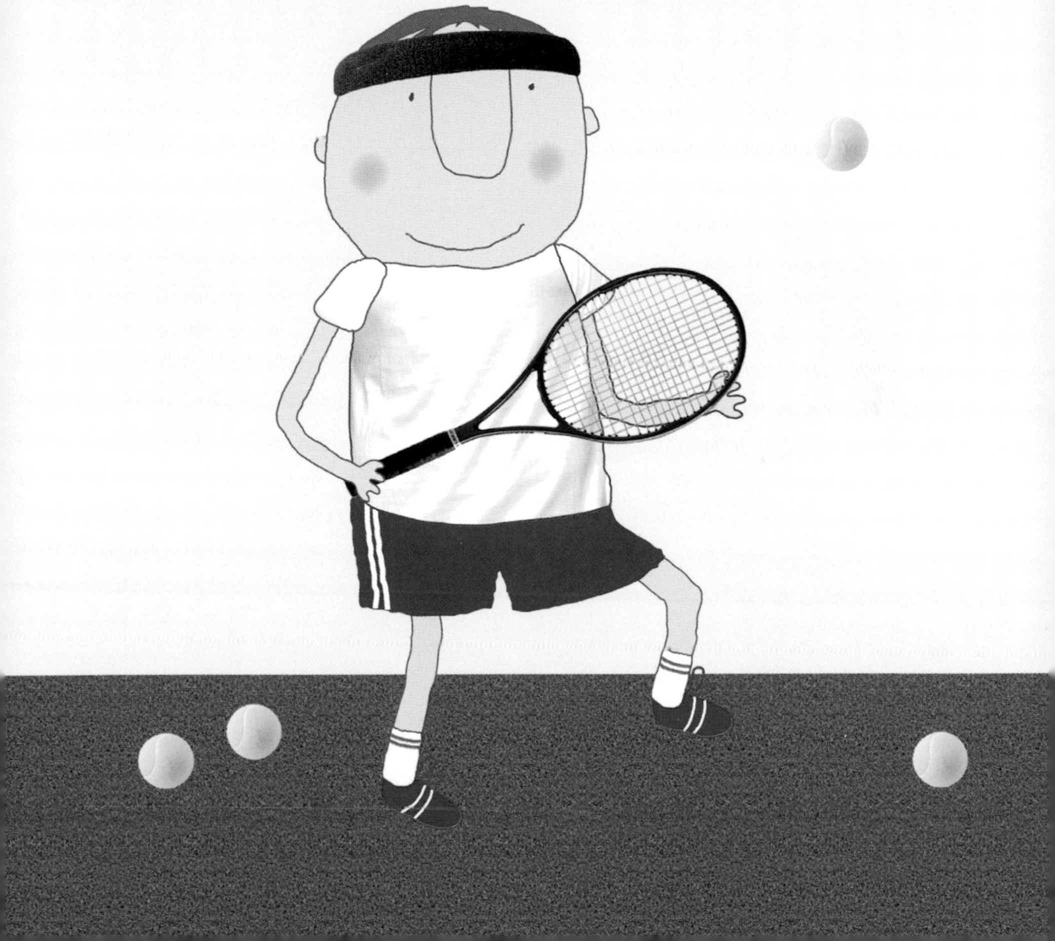

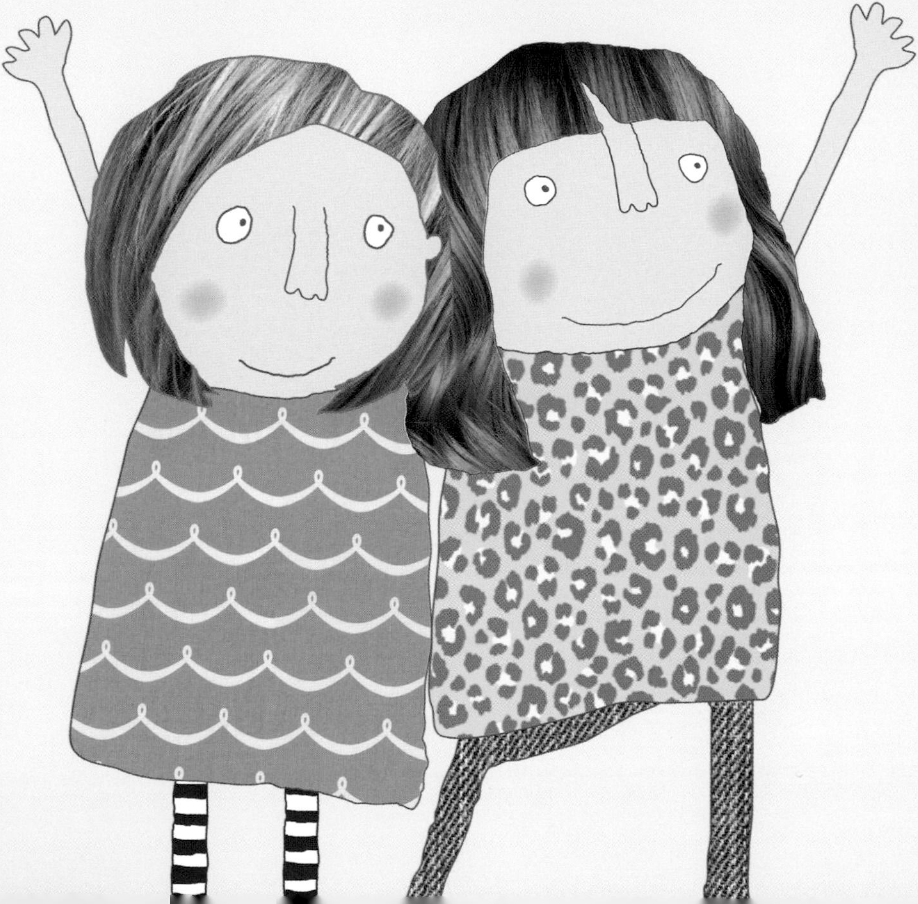

Besties

If my best friend laughs, I laugh

If she cries, I cry

If she falls, I laugh

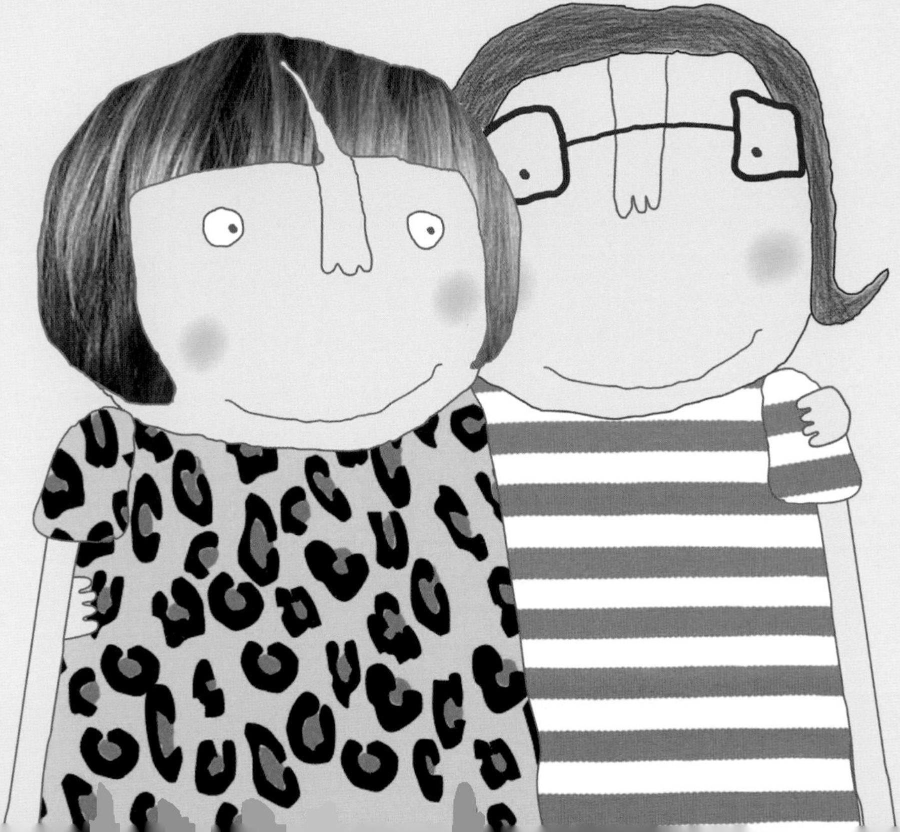

If you love a friend, let them go

If they come back with coffee and cake,
it was meant to be

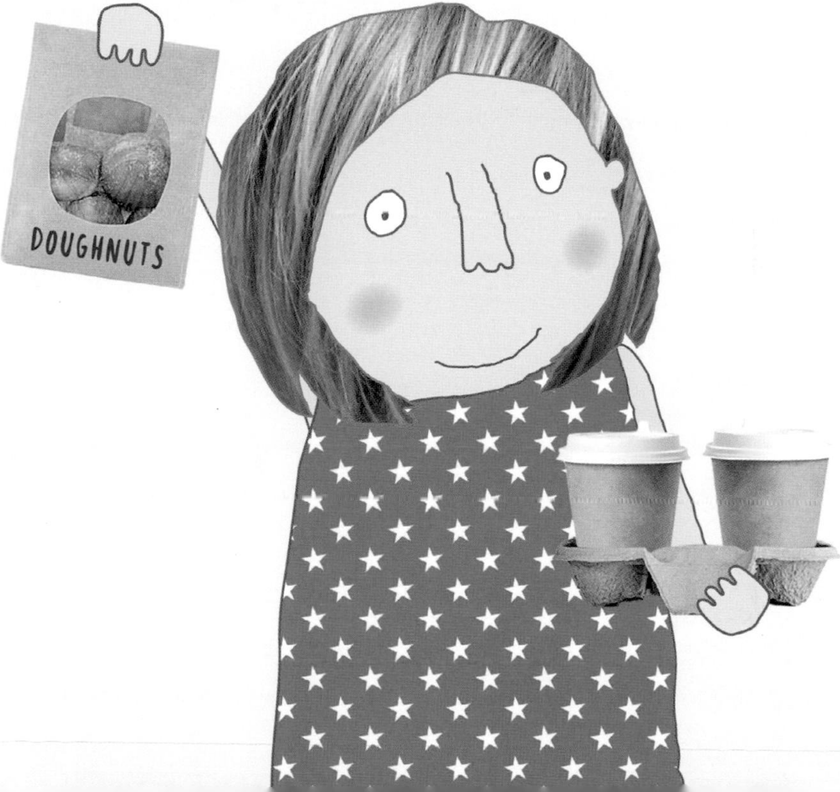
DOUGHNUTS

I feel sorry for people
who don't get to listen to our
conversations and enjoy our hilariousness

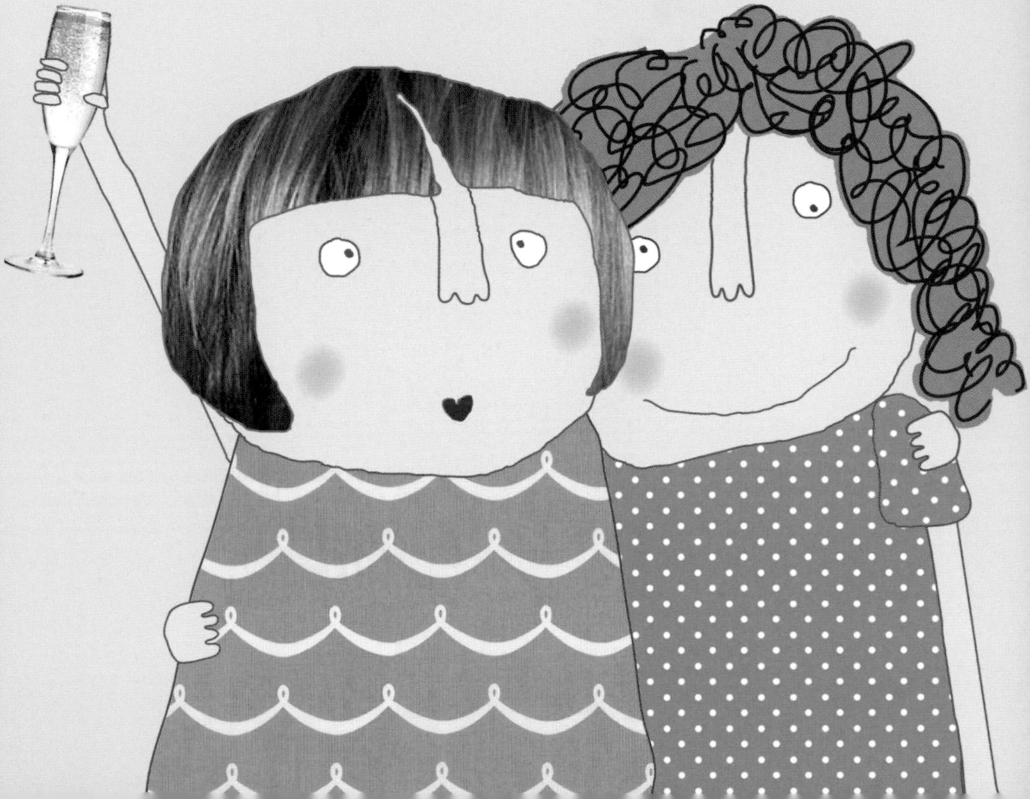

We all have that one friend who's bad for our liver

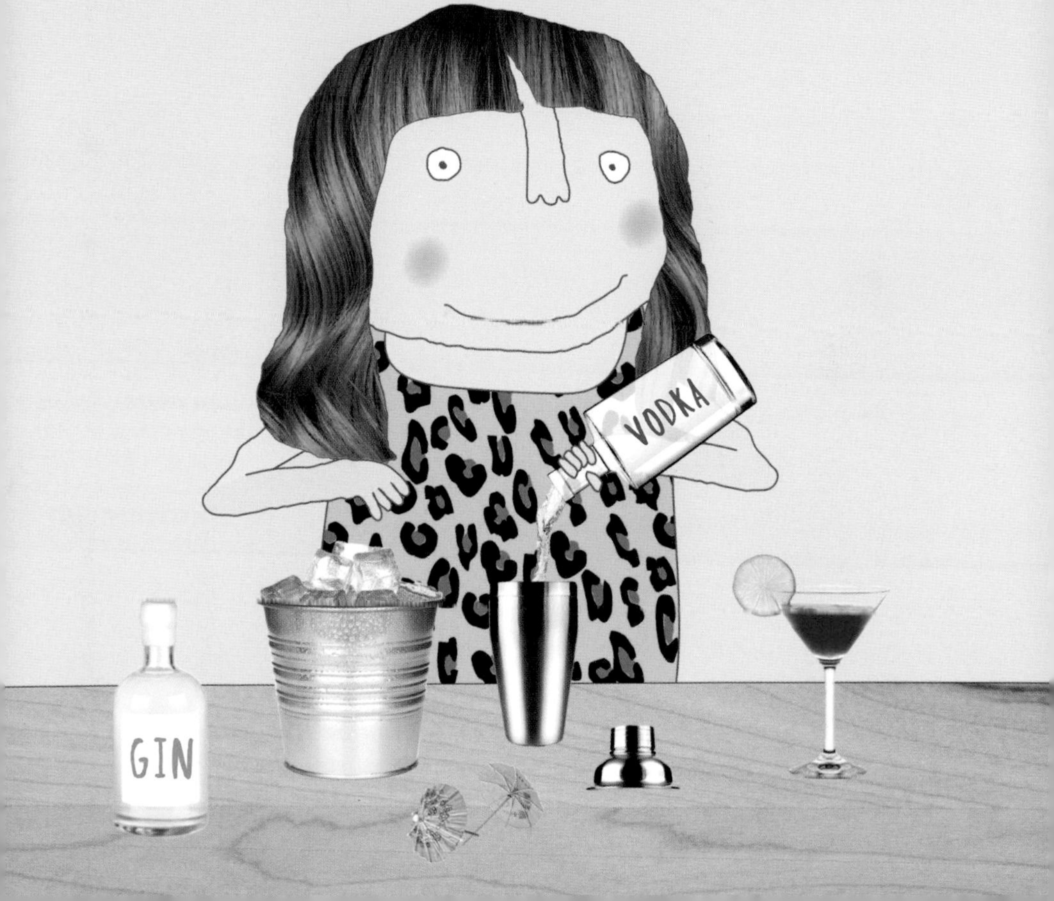
VODKA
GIN

Prosecco squad

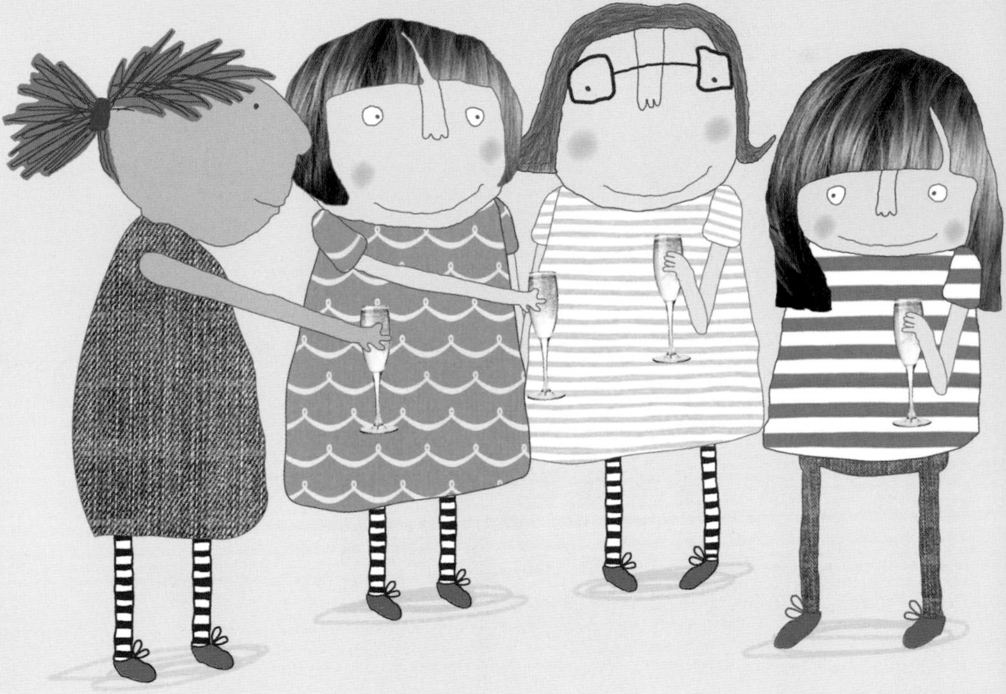

A true friend reaches for your hand

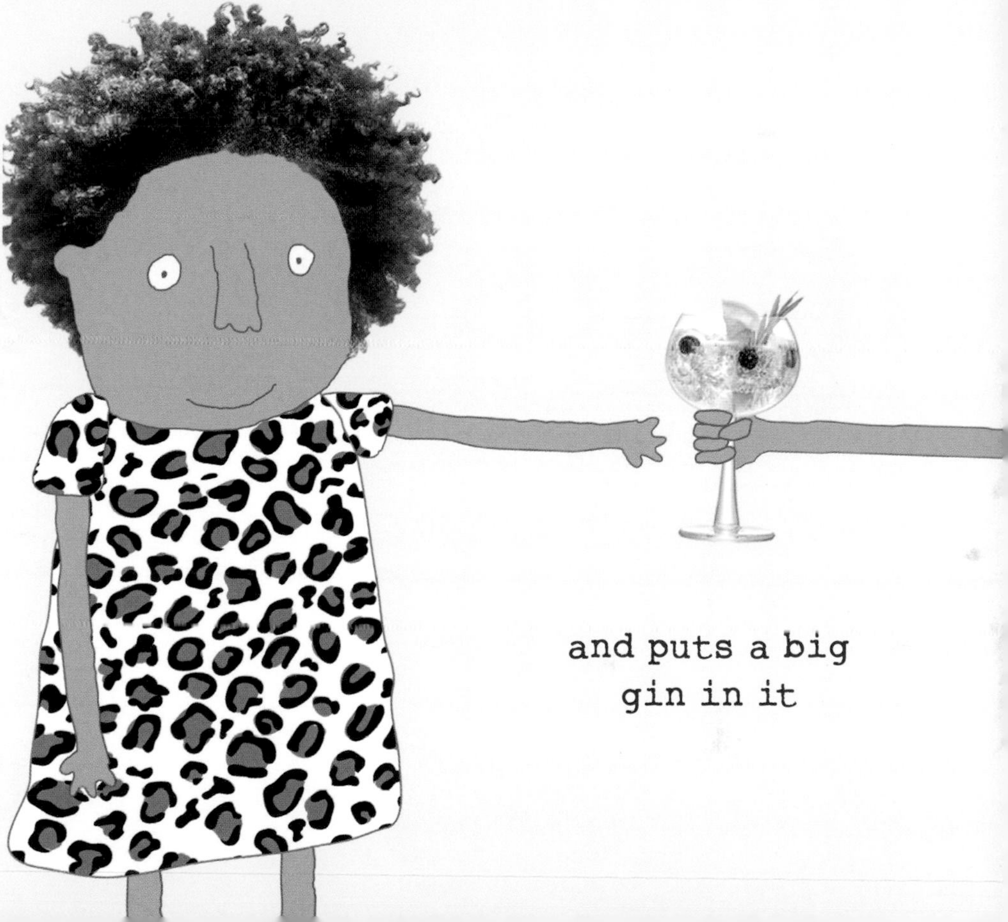

and puts a big gin in it

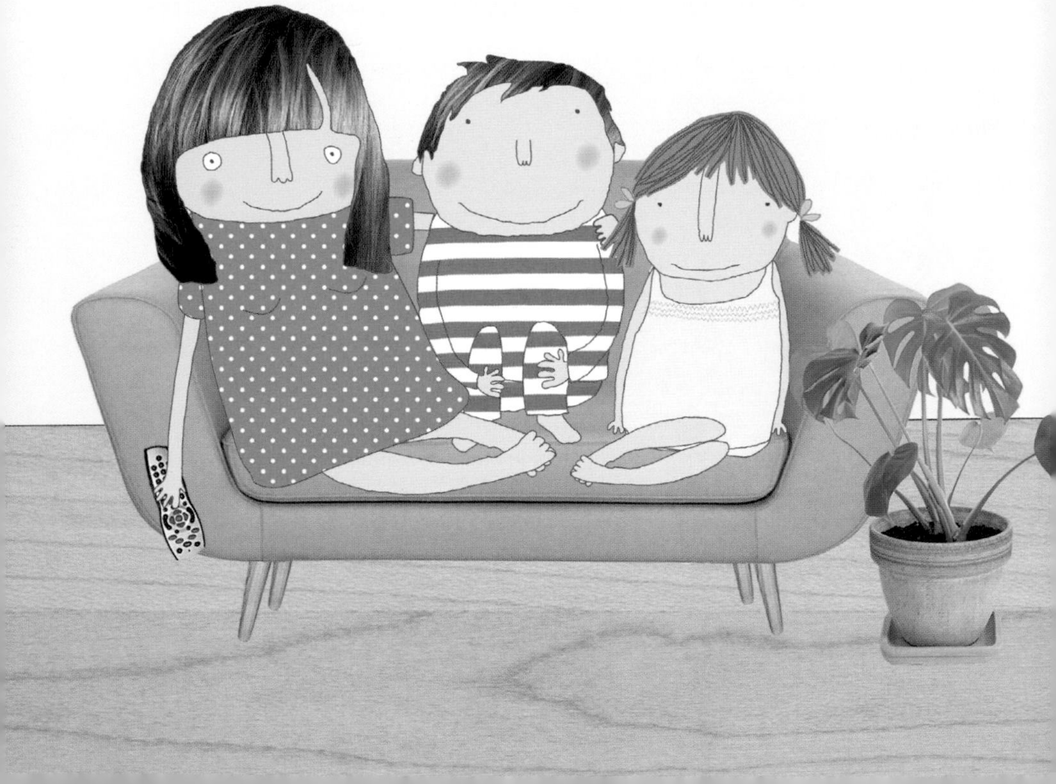

We are family

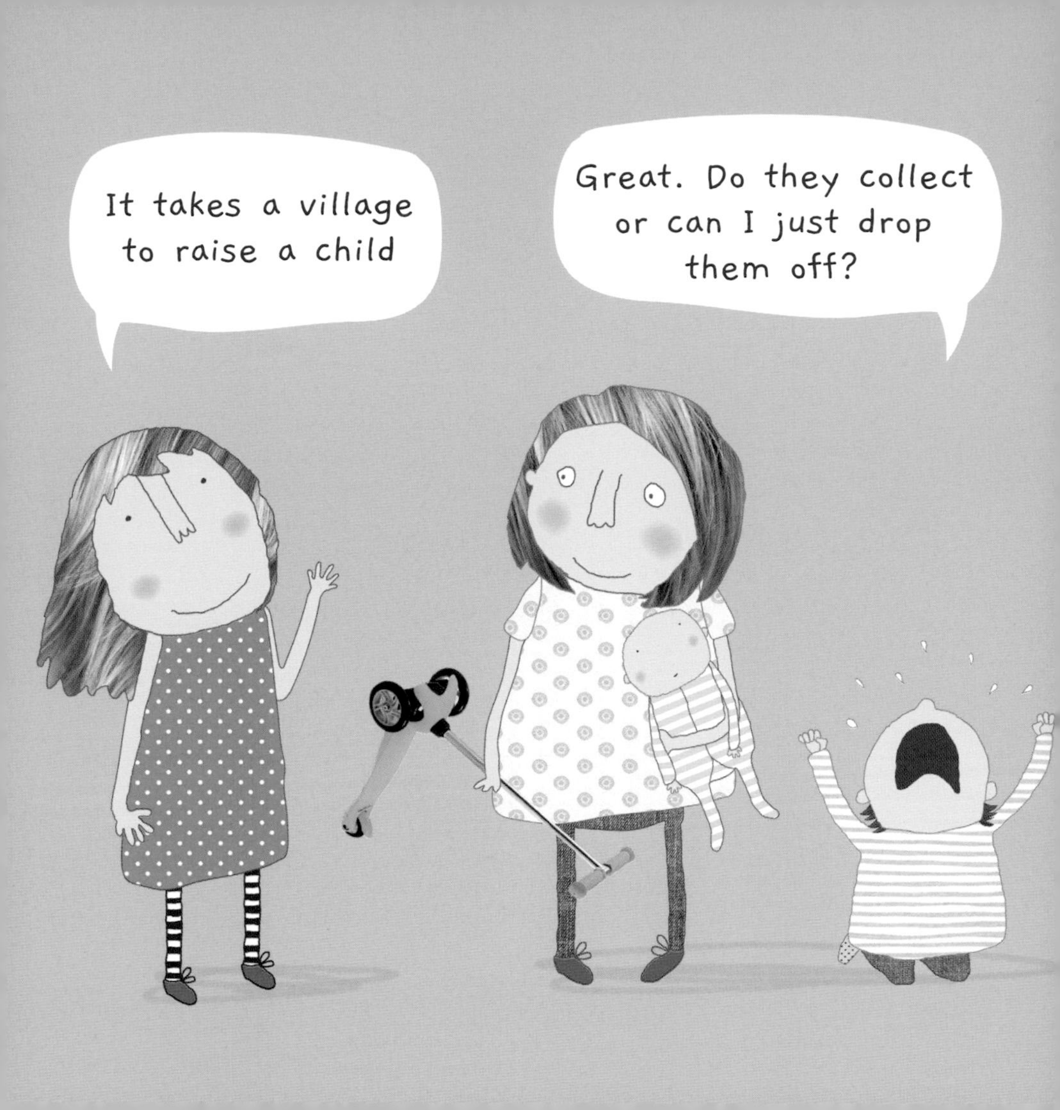
It takes a village to raise a child
Great. Do they collect or can I just drop them off?

If a man says you're ugly, he's just mean

If a woman says you're ugly, she's jealous

If a kid says you're ugly,
you're ugly

I never knew how annoying I could be
until I created a mini version of myself
and argued with it daily

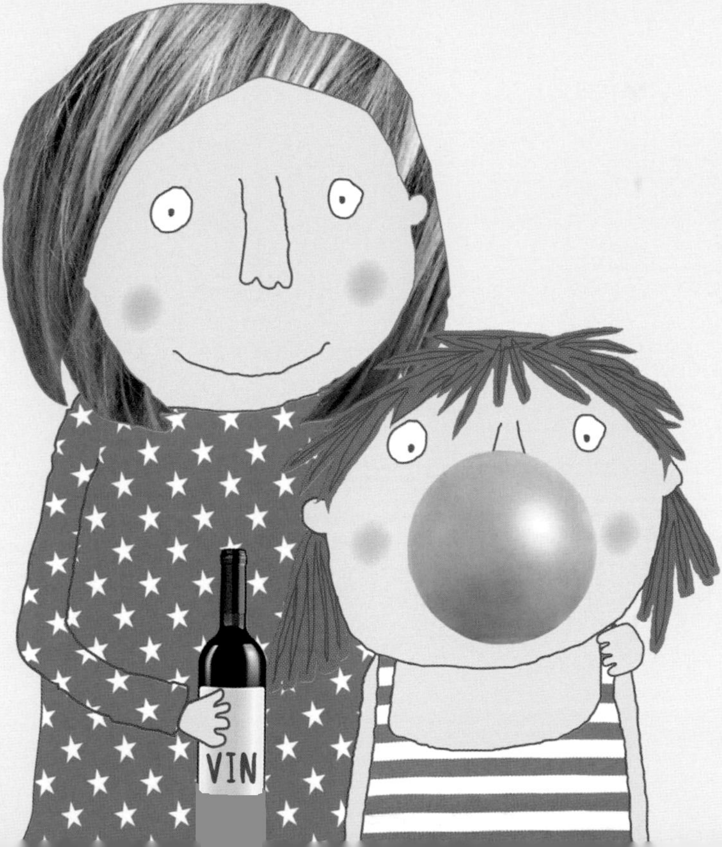
VIN

Mum flu

Like man flu but no one gives a shit

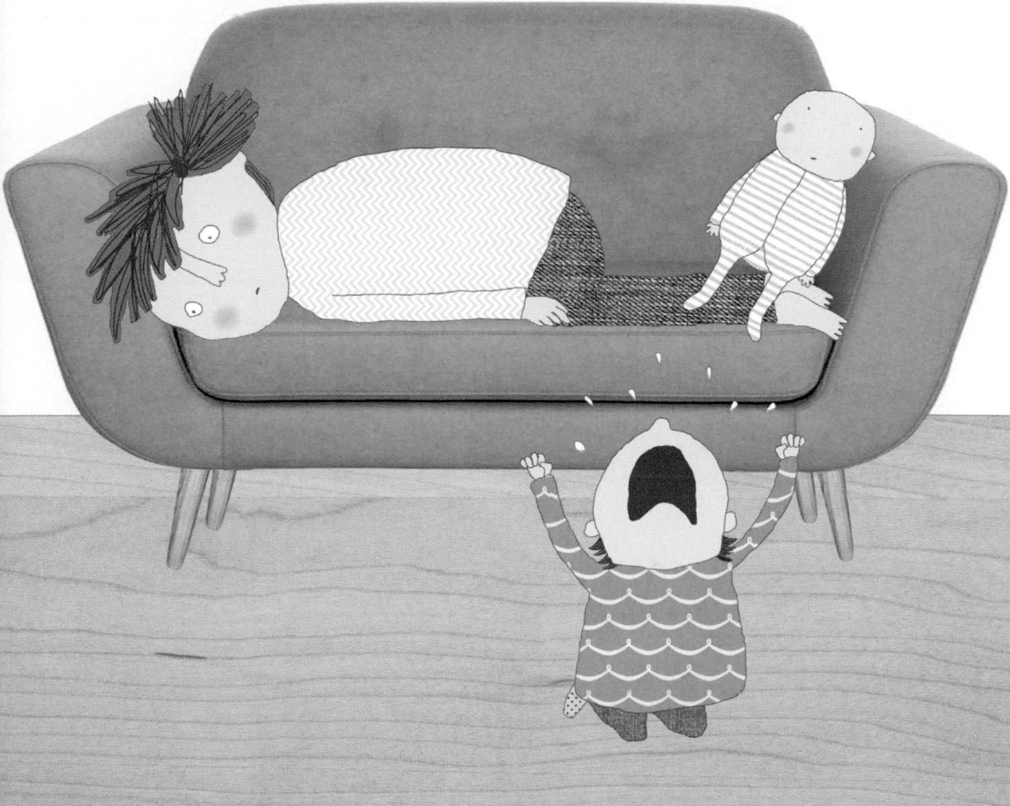

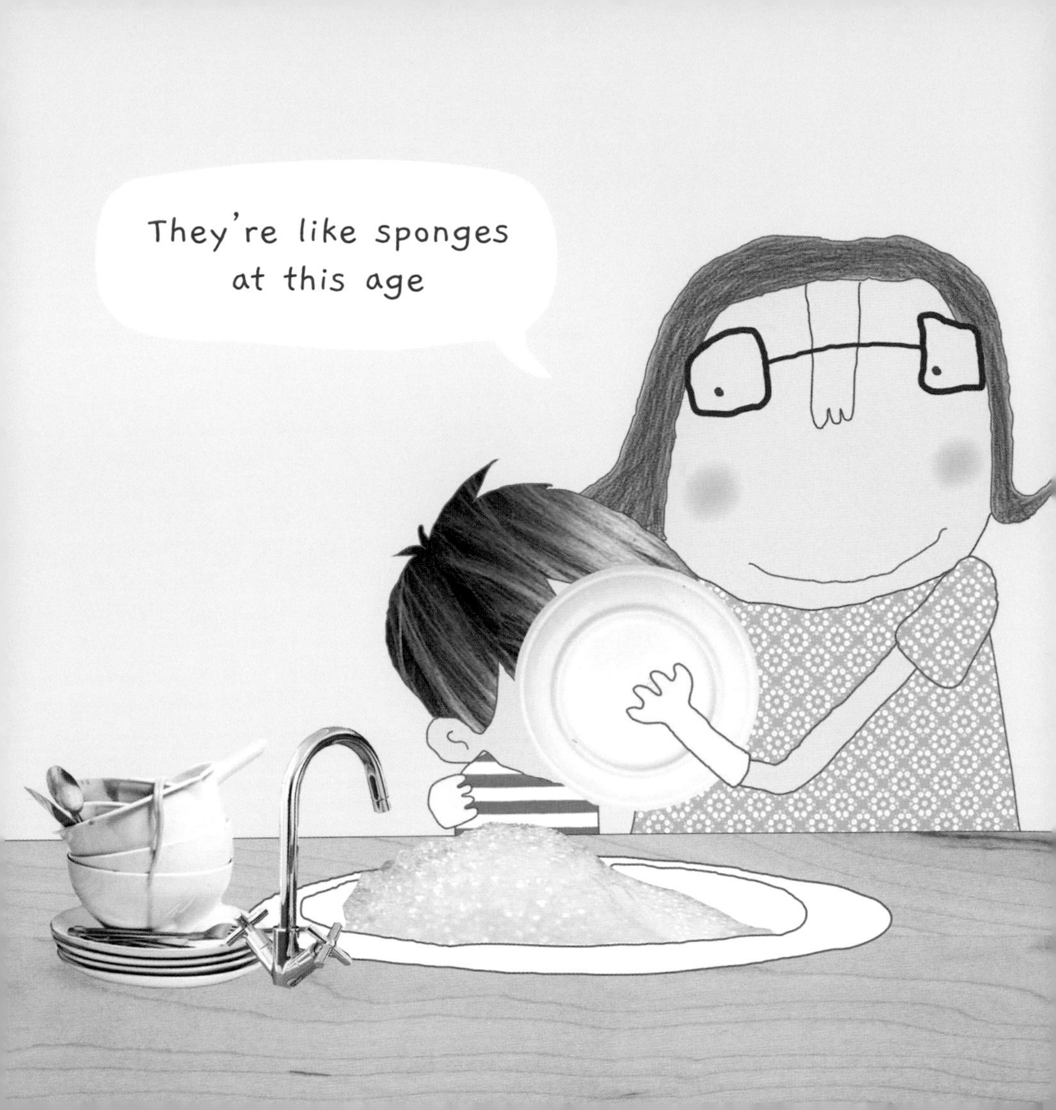
They're like sponges at this age

Netflix & Chil...dren

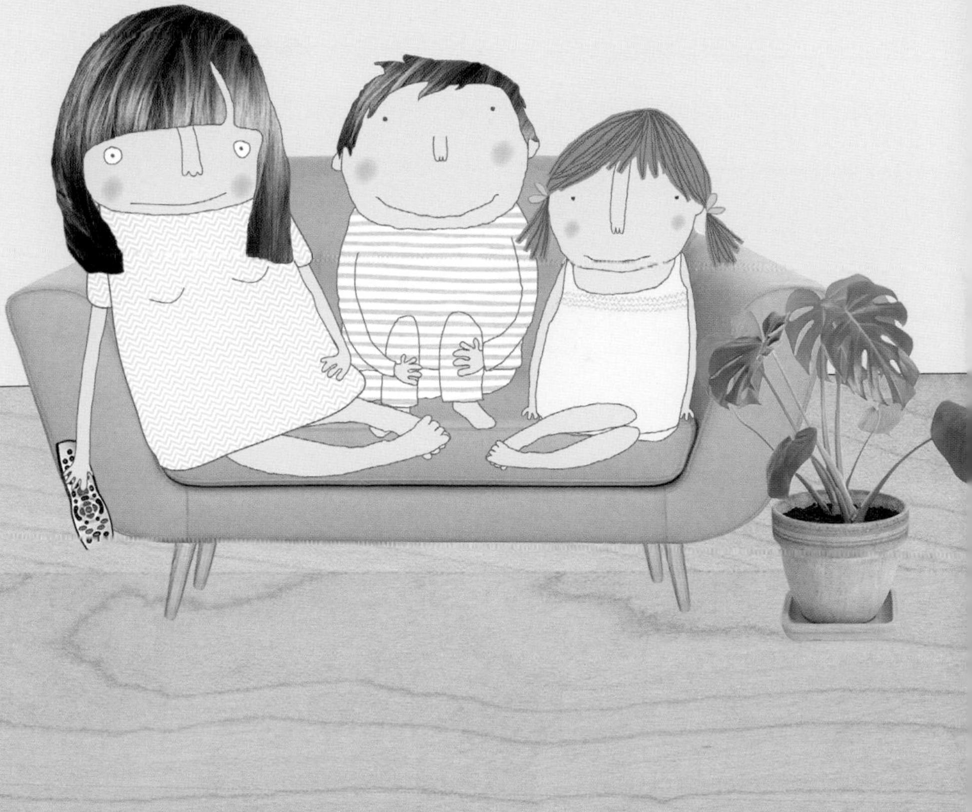

We decided to have another child because Poppy's just not pulling the likes on Facebook like she used to

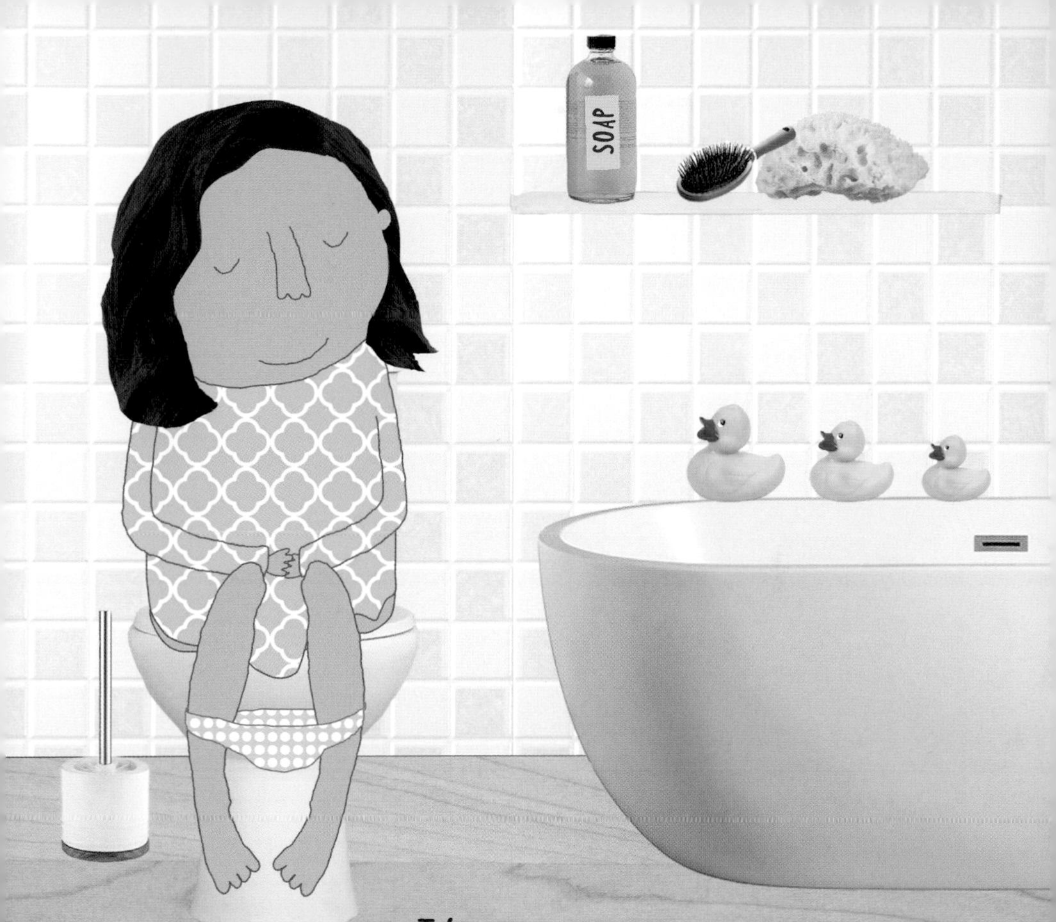
SOAP

I'm a mum
My hobbies include silence
and going to the toilet alone

Me, being the fun summer mum I promised myself I'd be this year

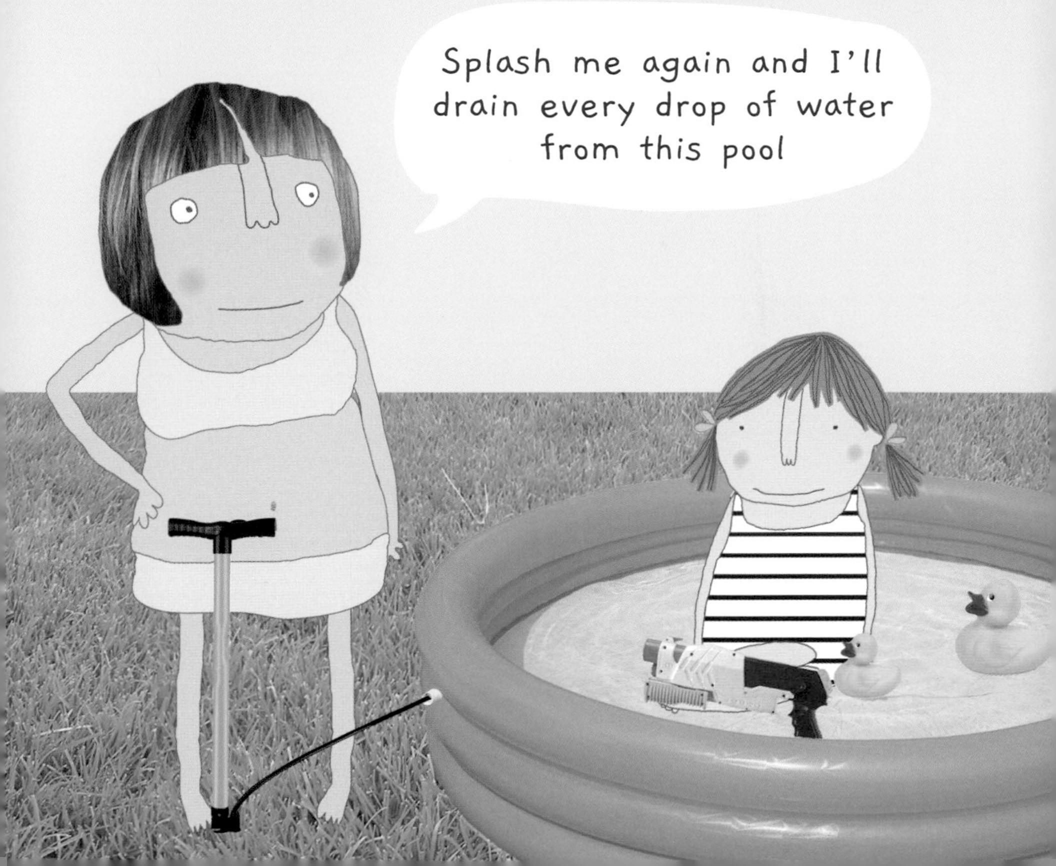
Splash me again and I'll drain every drop of water from this pool

Parents, recreate that Center Parcs holiday this half-term by watching your children cycle round the garden in the rain whilst burning £20 notes

I'm sorry I kept you awake last night

Not really. I don't care.

If you enjoy eating cold food
whilst standing over a bin...

I can't recommend
parenthood enough

You've put the kids in bed
Now you can finally...

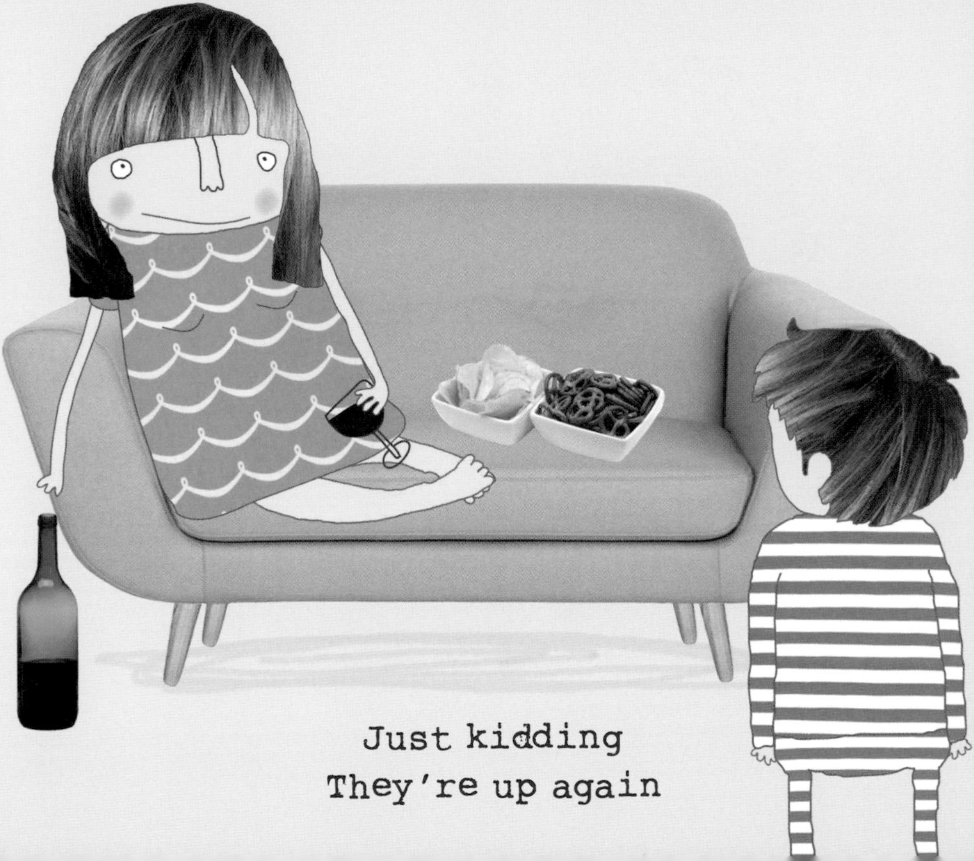

Just kidding
They're up again

Fun new drinking game for parents

Take a shot every time your child moans

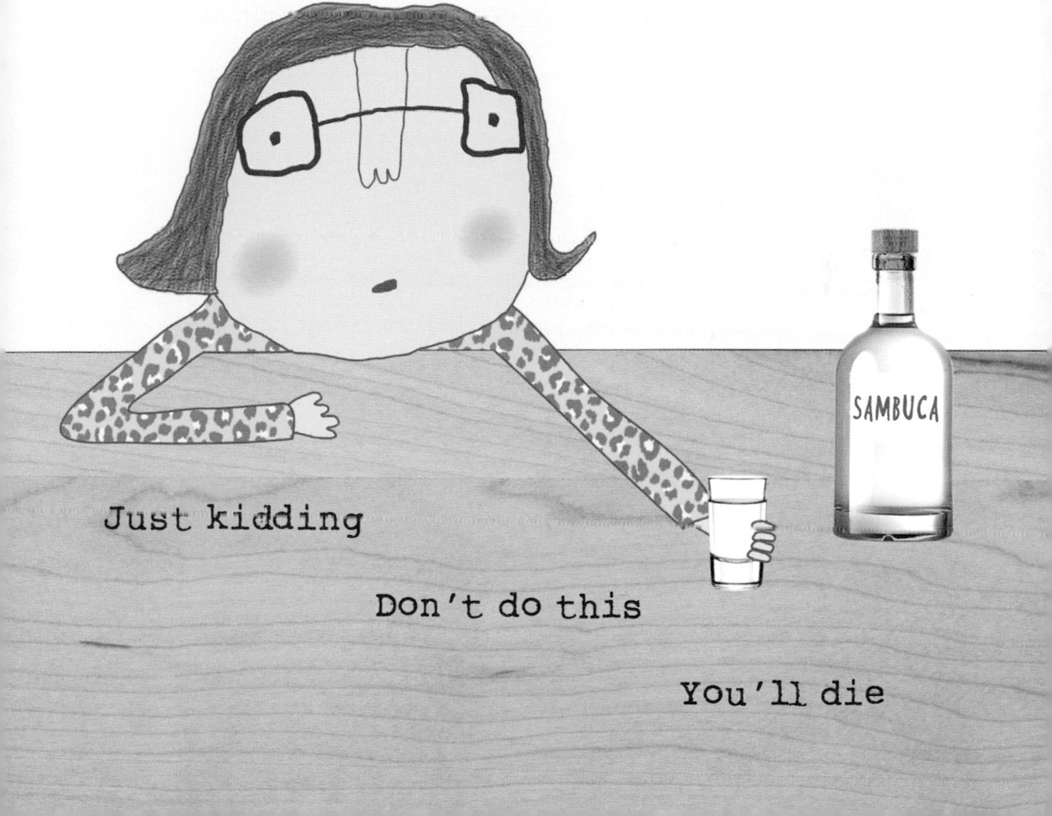
SAMBUCA
Just kidding
Don't do this
You'll die

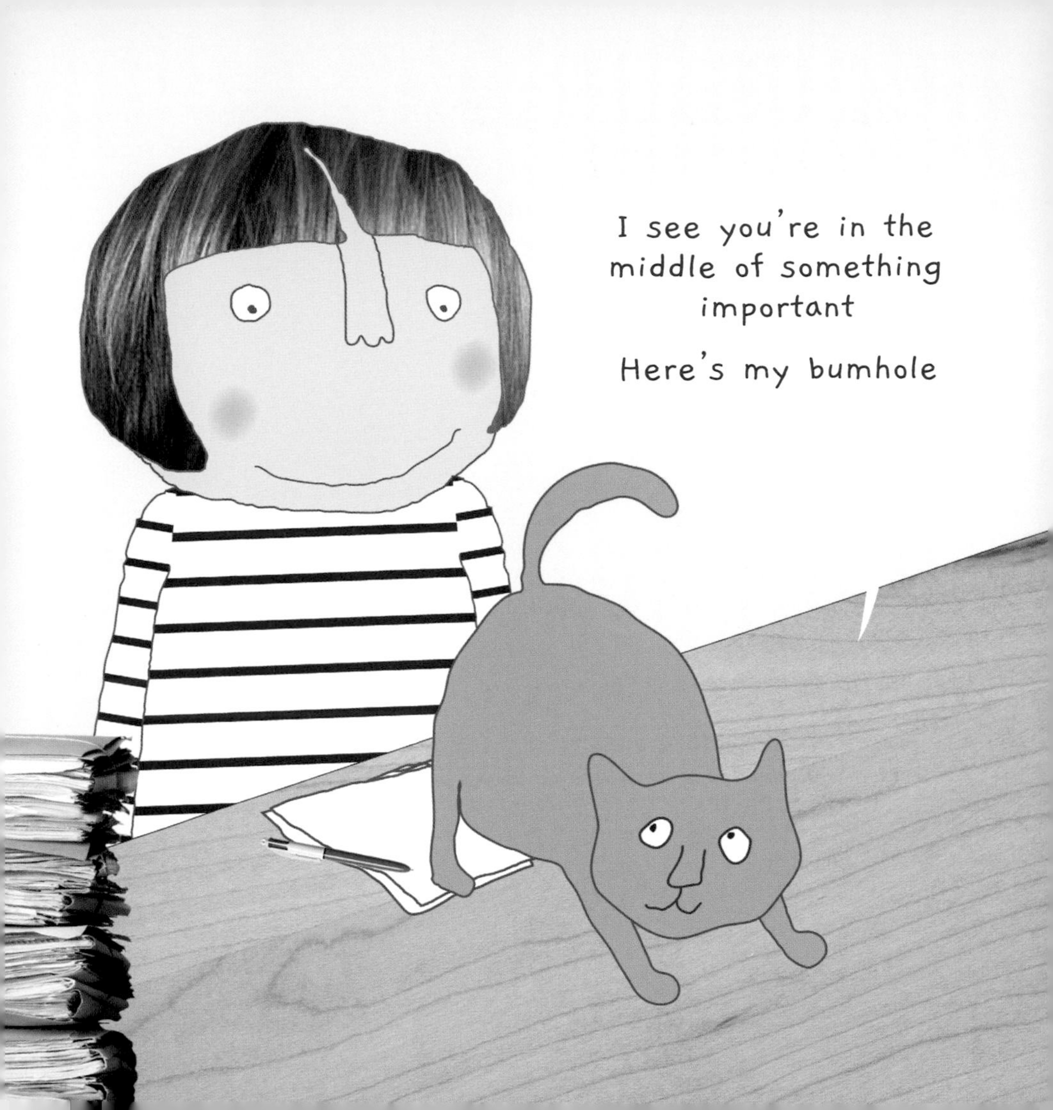
I see you're in the middle of something important
Here's my bumhole

There is no greater love than that between a grumpy dad and the pet they said they didn't want

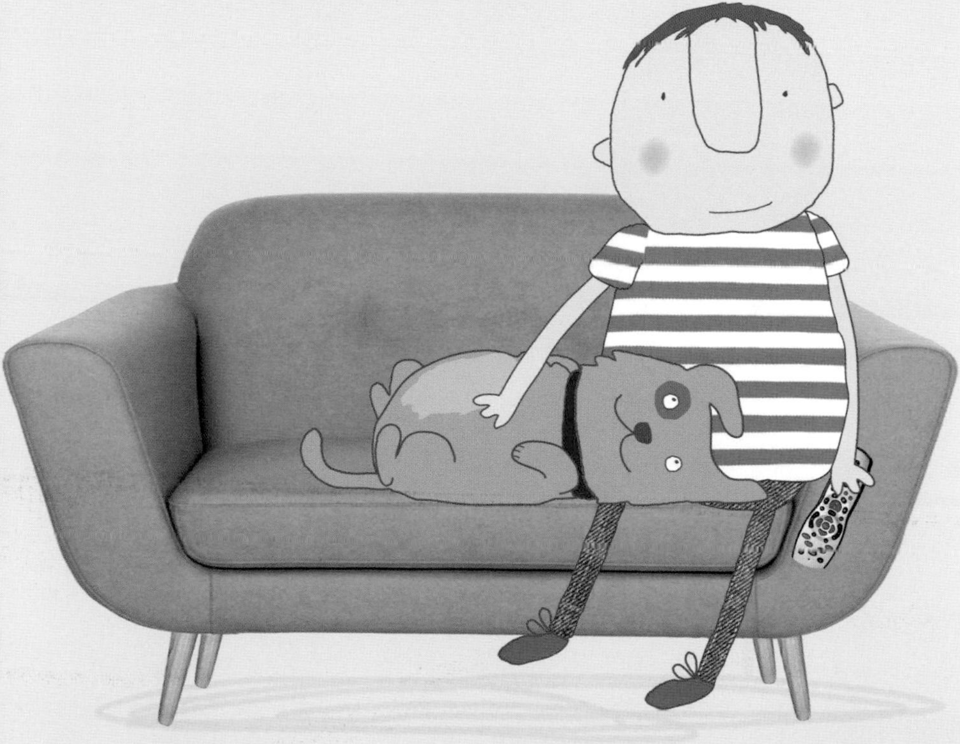

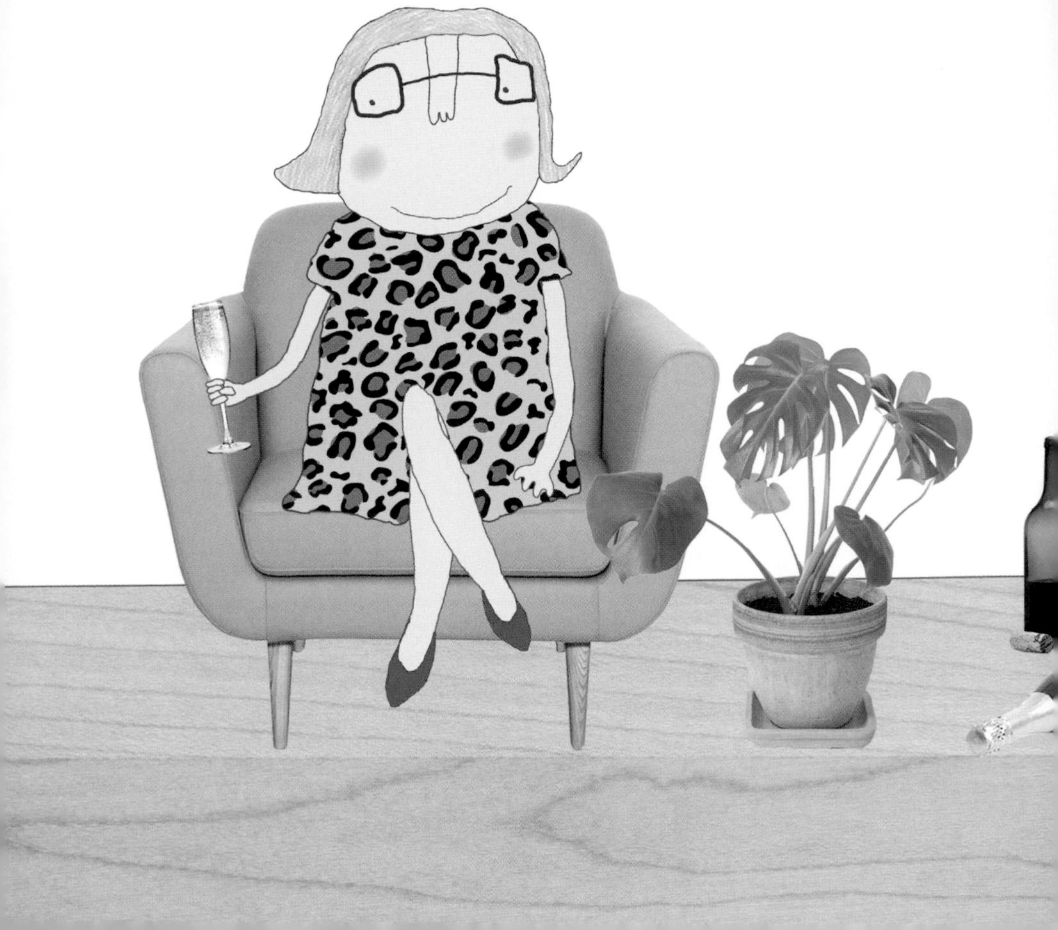

Domestic goddess

I found a spider in my bath...

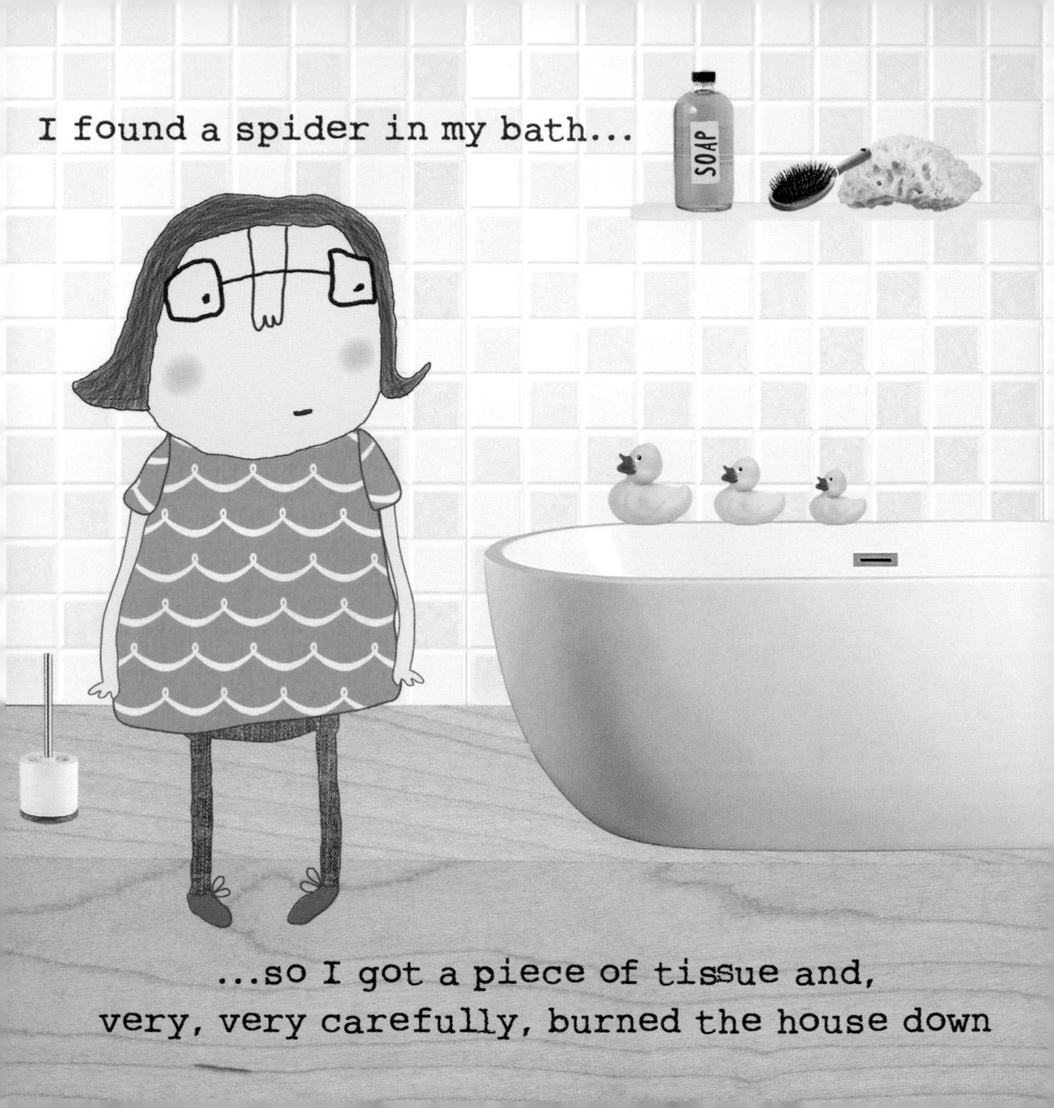
SOAP

...so I got a piece of tissue and,
very, very carefully, burned the house down

Sometimes you might feel like
there's no one there for you but
you know who's always there for you?

Laundry

Laundry will always
be there for you

One day you're young and trendy

The next you're impressed by someone's washer/dryer situation

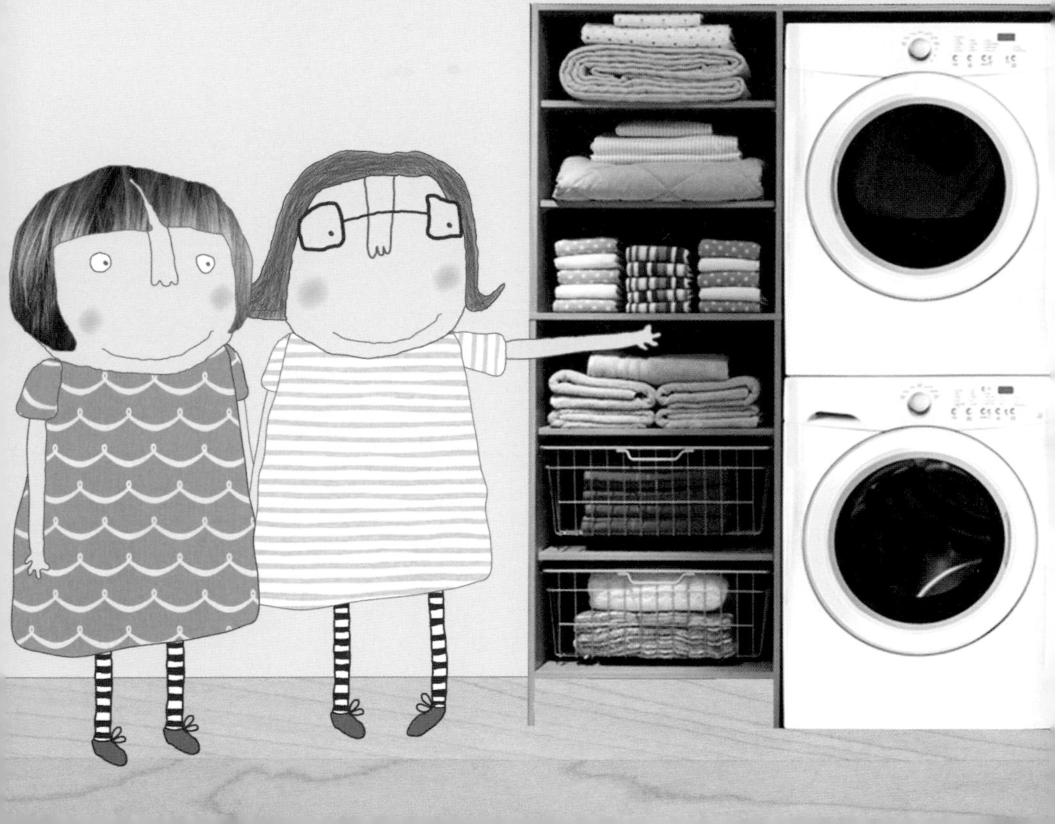

Marriage is just your spouse perpetually standing in front of the kitchen drawer or cupboard you need to open

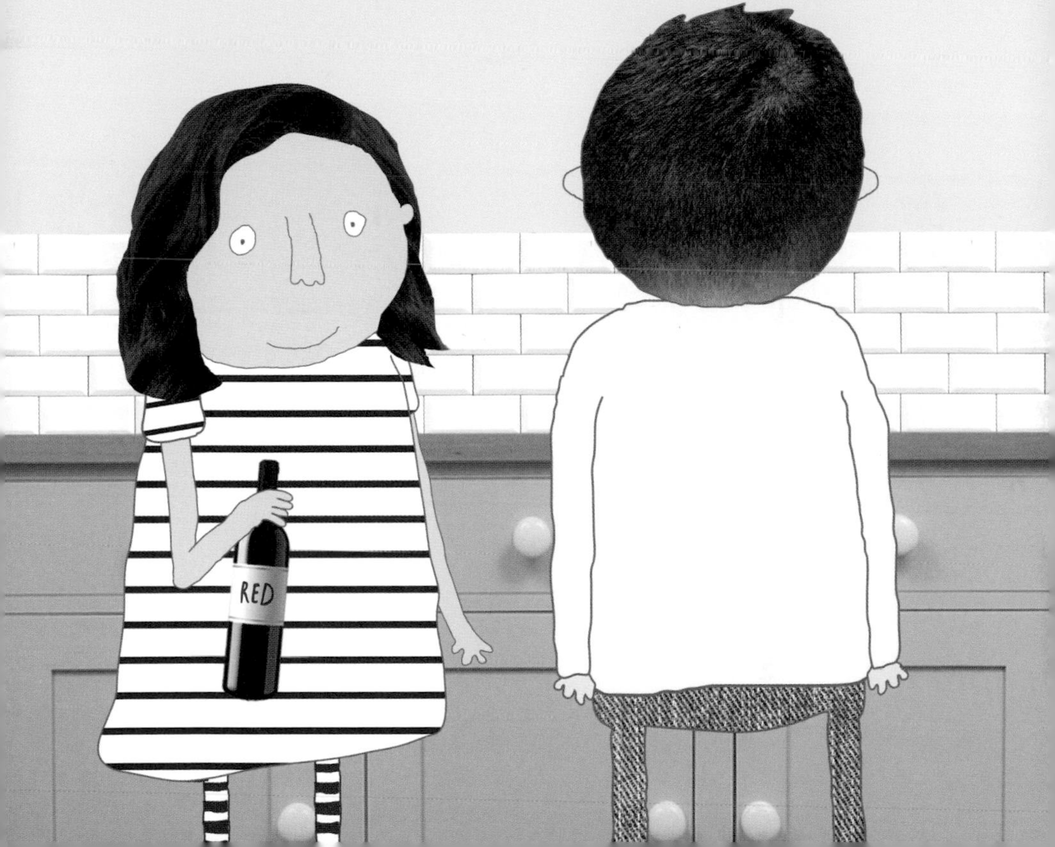
RED

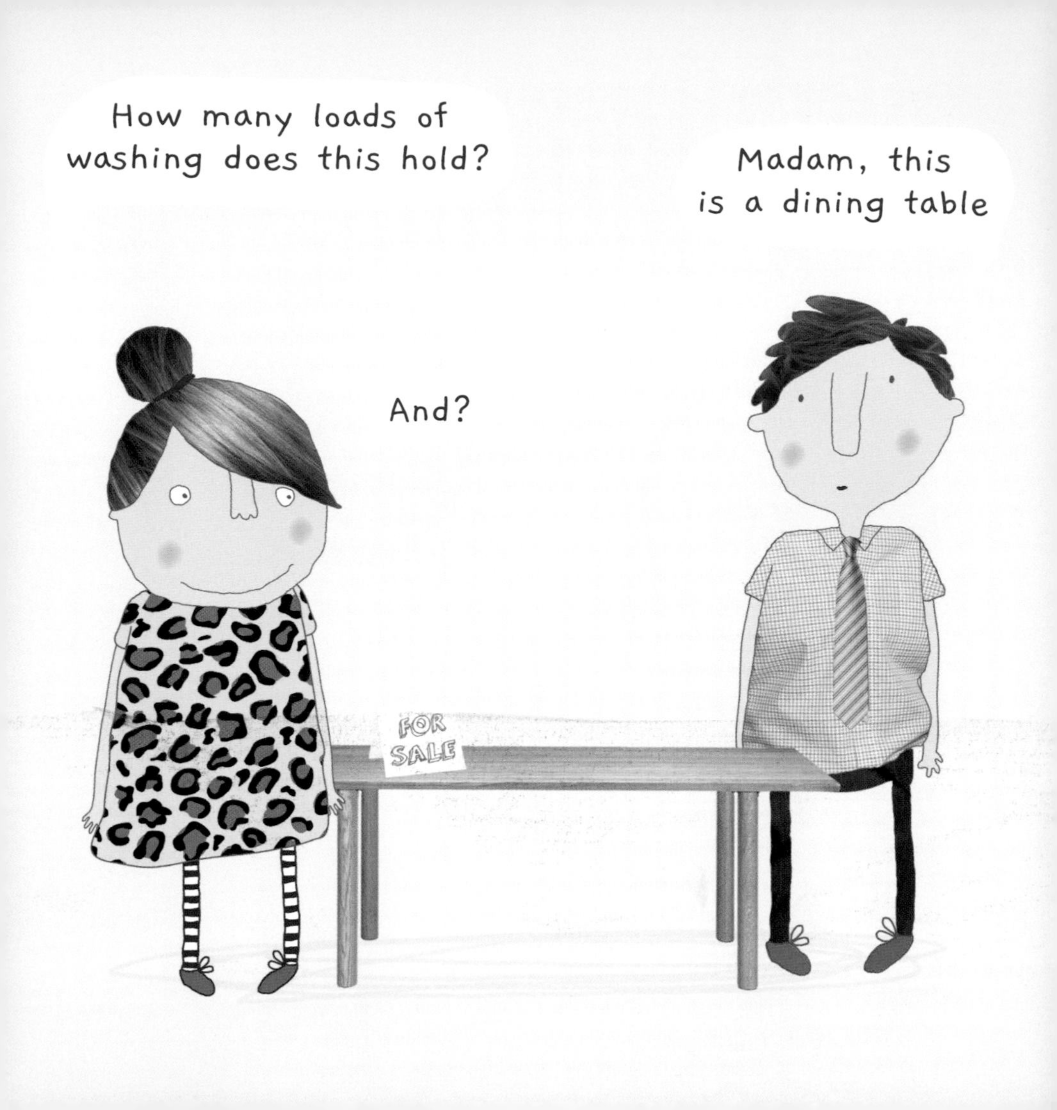
How many loads of washing does this hold?
Madam, this is a dining table
And?
FOR SALE

I fantasise about having two men at once

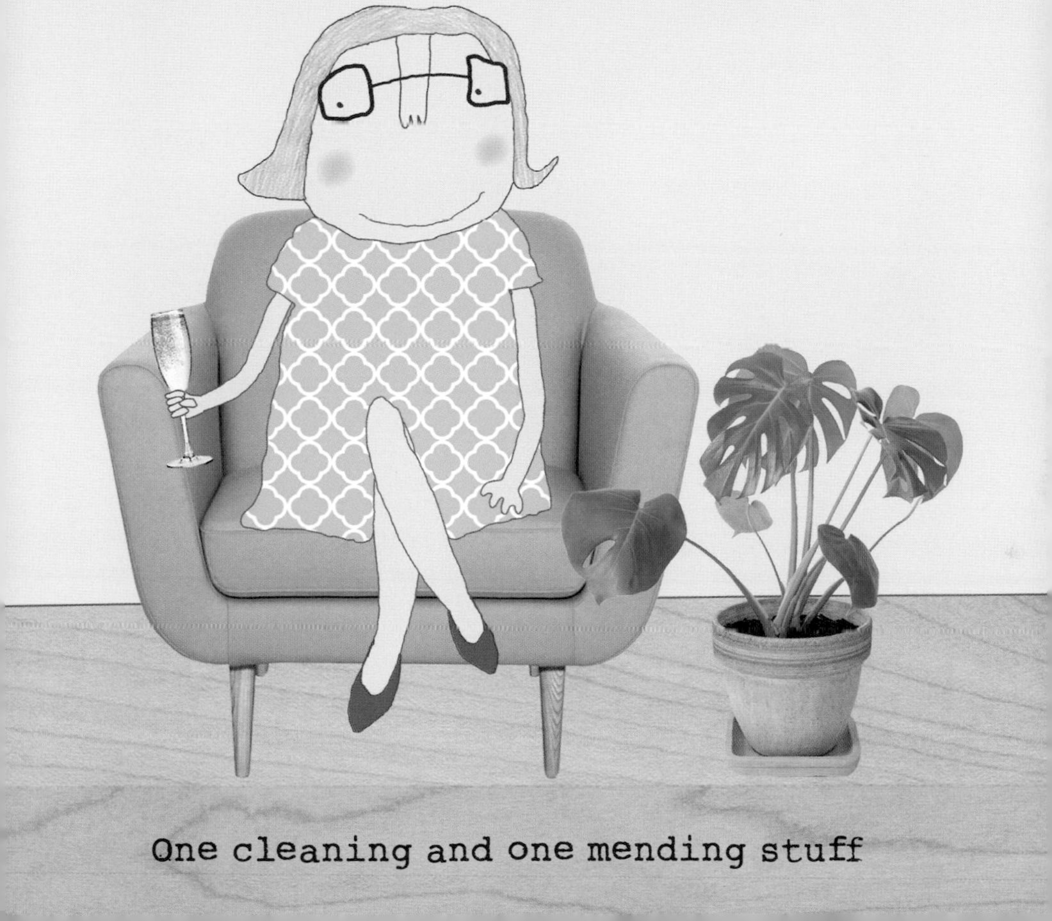

One cleaning and one mending stuff

This is a lot of
days in a row to
have to make dinner

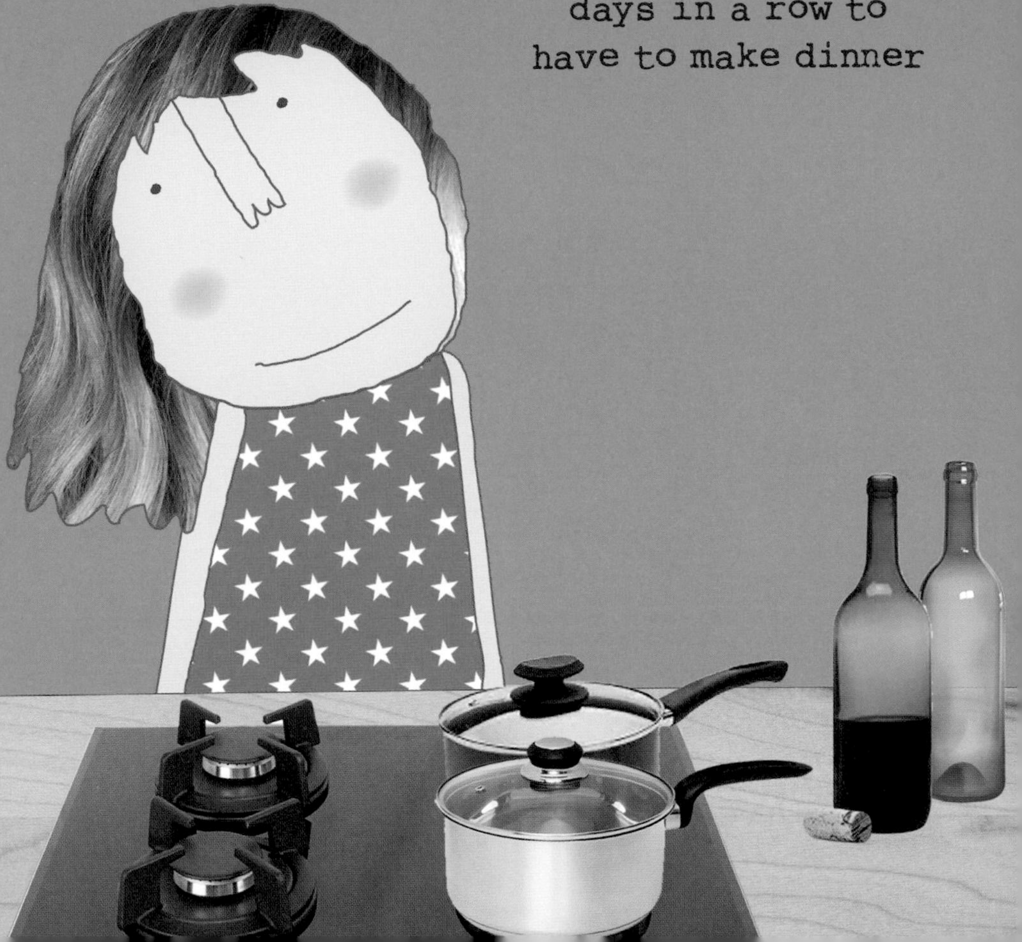

Follow me for more recipes

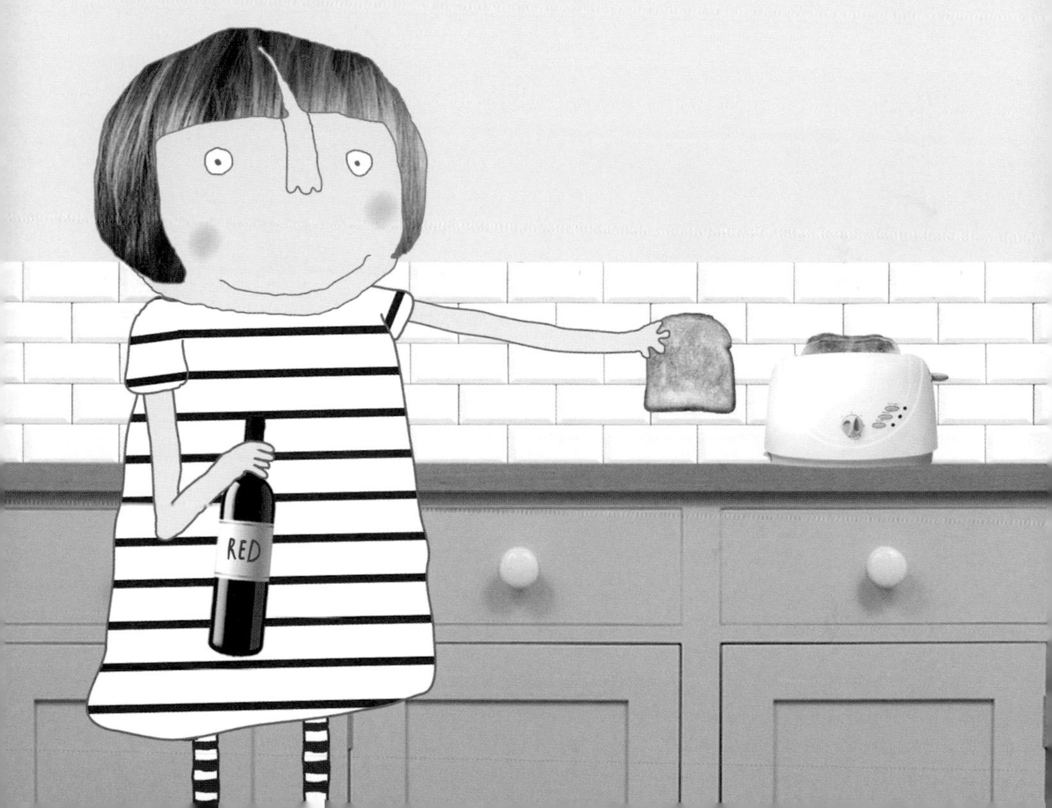
RED

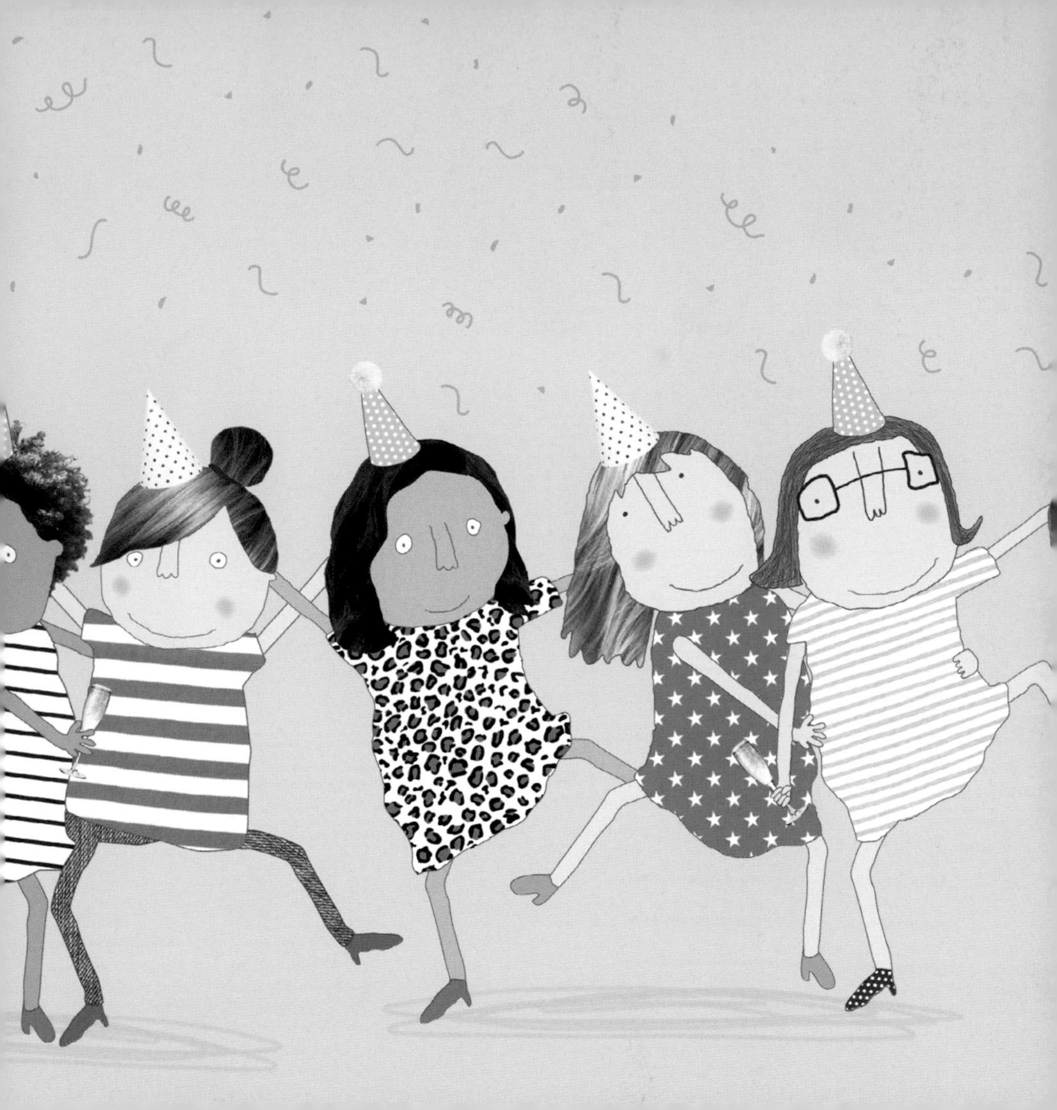

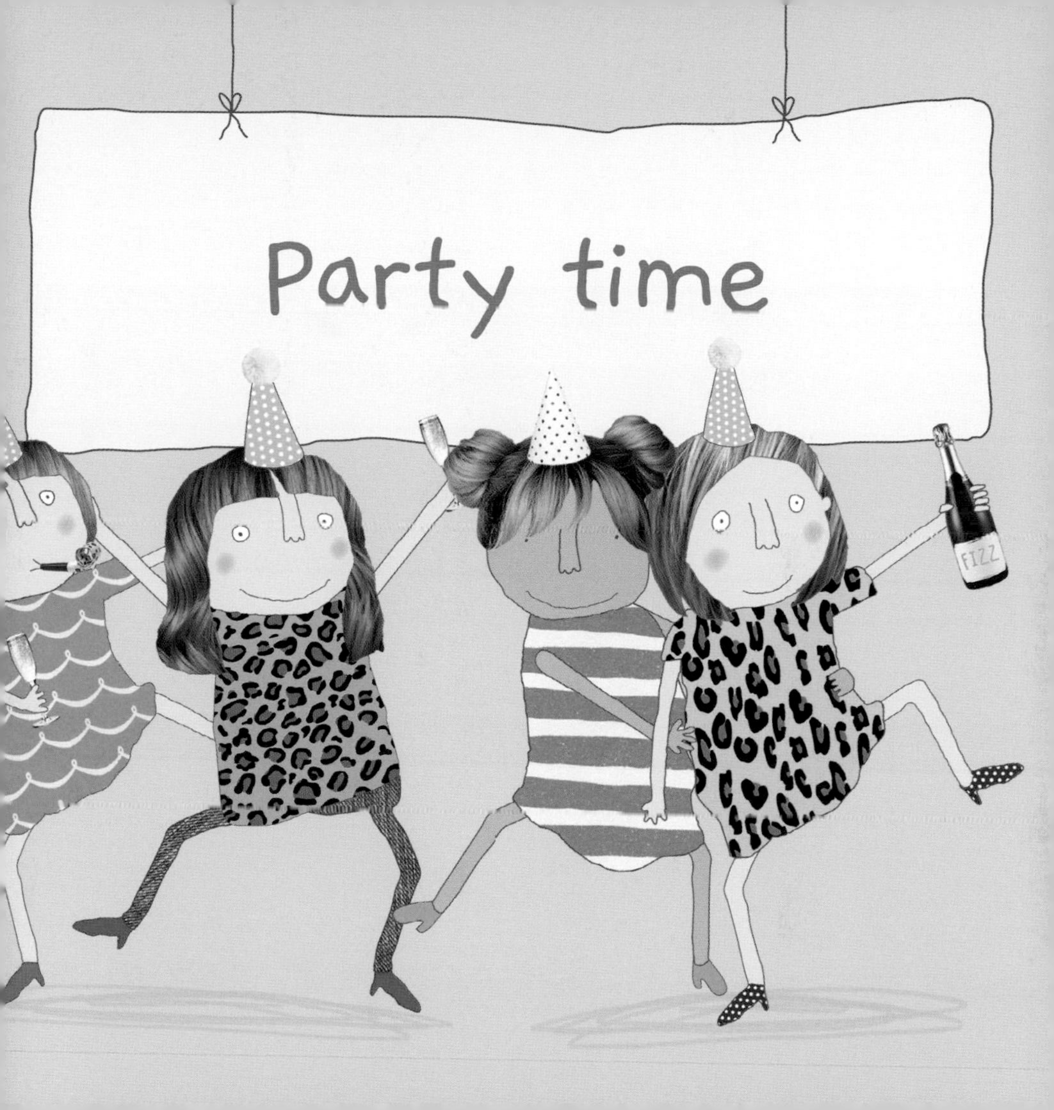
Party time
FIZZ

Maybe she's born with it

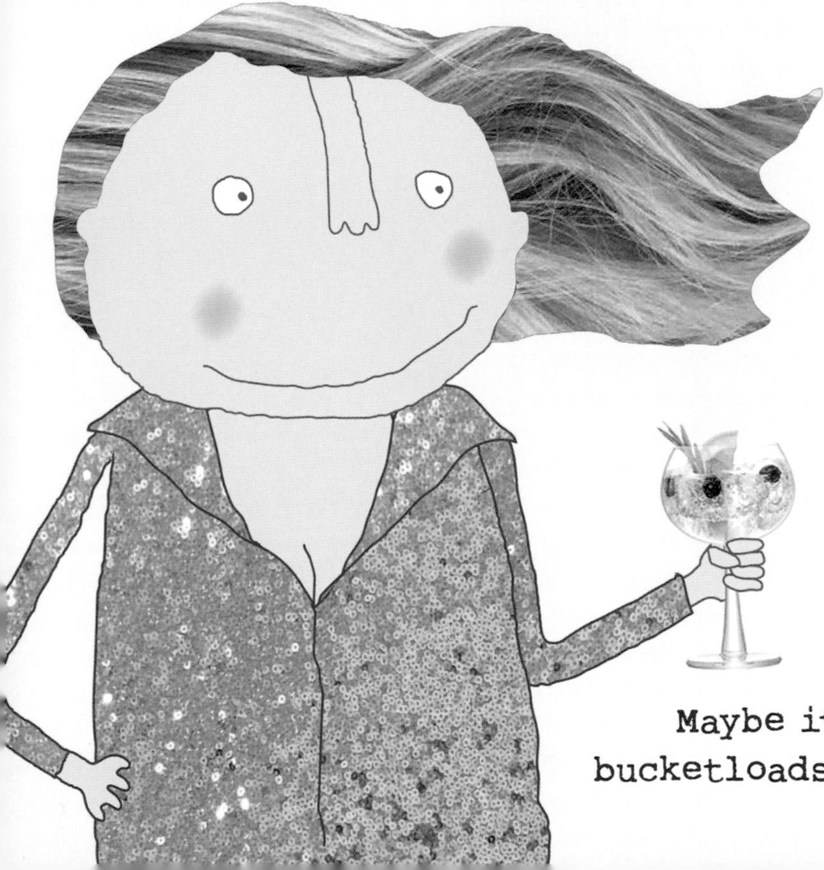

Maybe it's
bucketloads of gin

There's a responsible adult in all of us

But we can usually shut her up with a mojito

ESPRESSO MARTINI

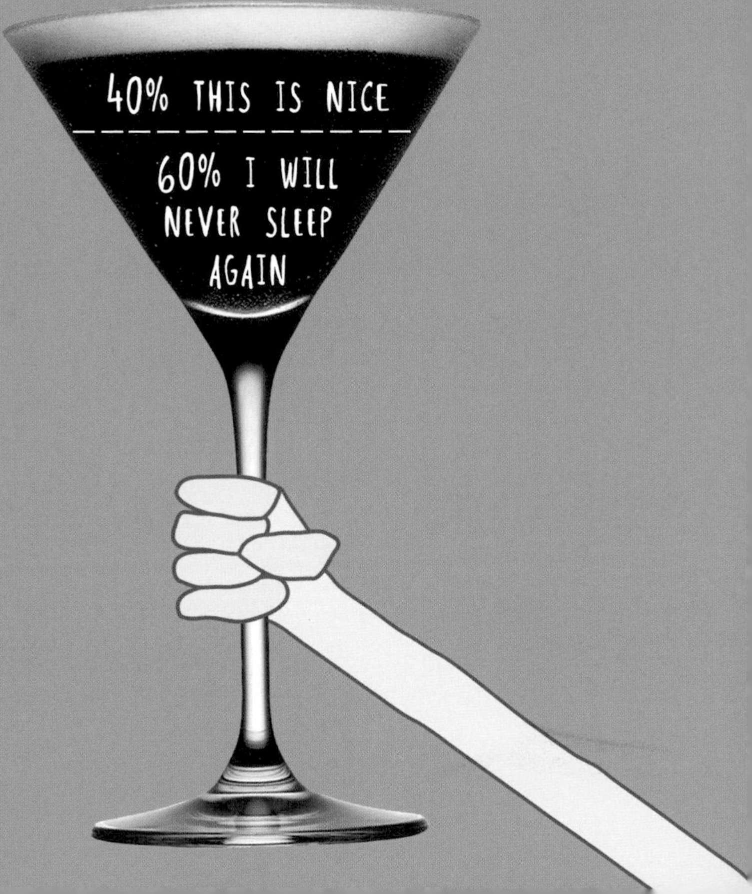
40% THIS IS NICE
60% I WILL NEVER SLEEP AGAIN

Never drink cocktails on an empty stomach

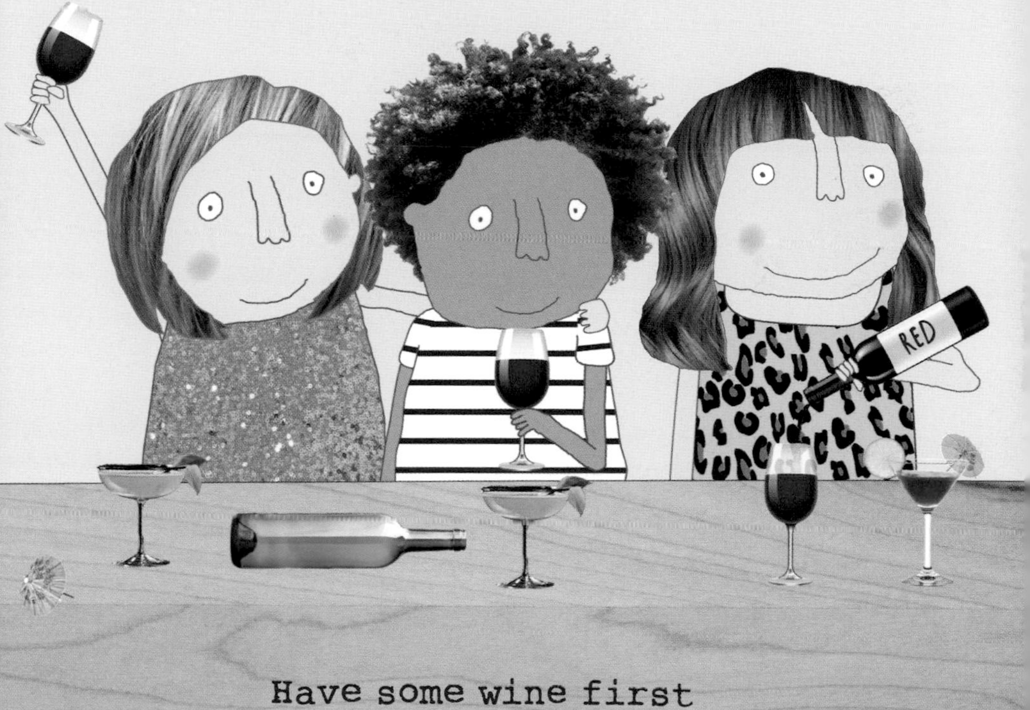
RED

Have some wine first

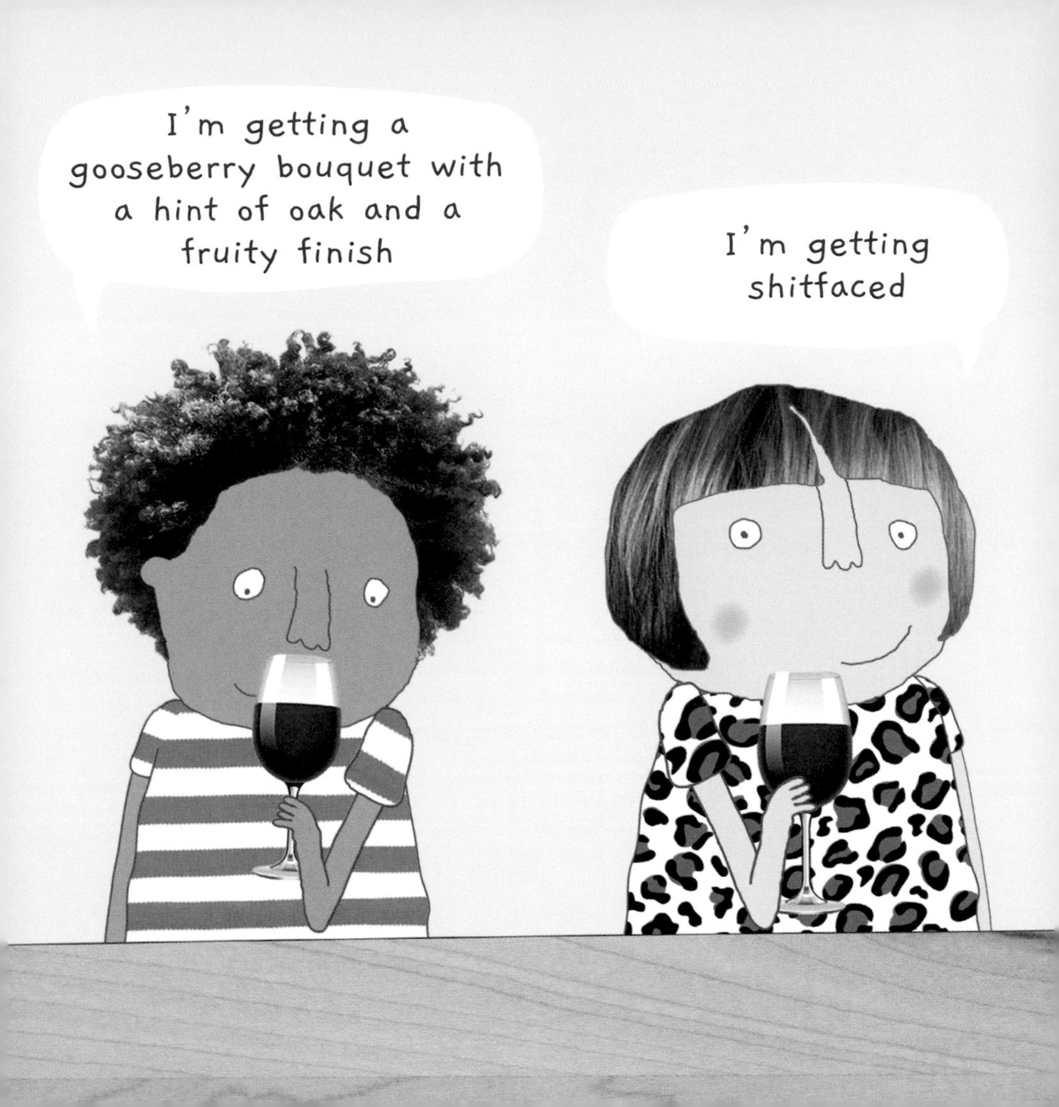
I'm getting a gooseberry bouquet with a hint of oak and a fruity finish
I'm getting shitfaced

Born to be wild

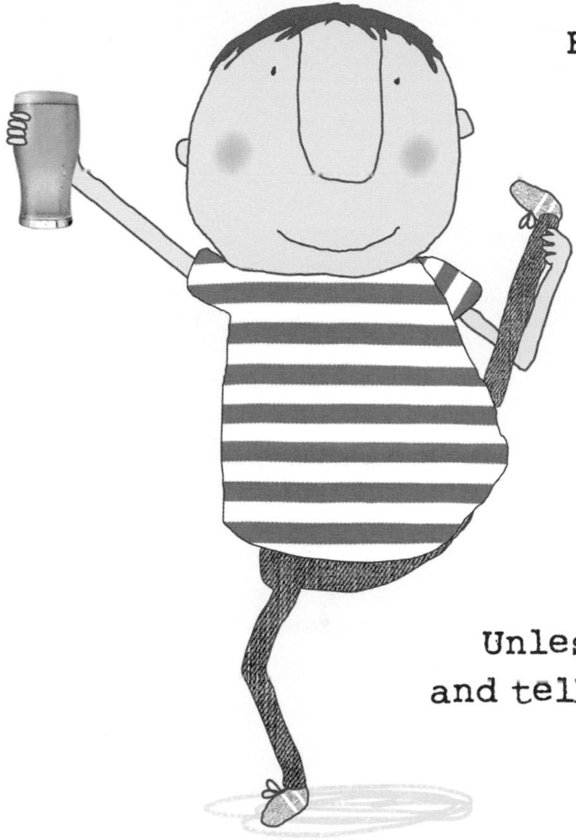

Unless my wife calls
and tells me to come home

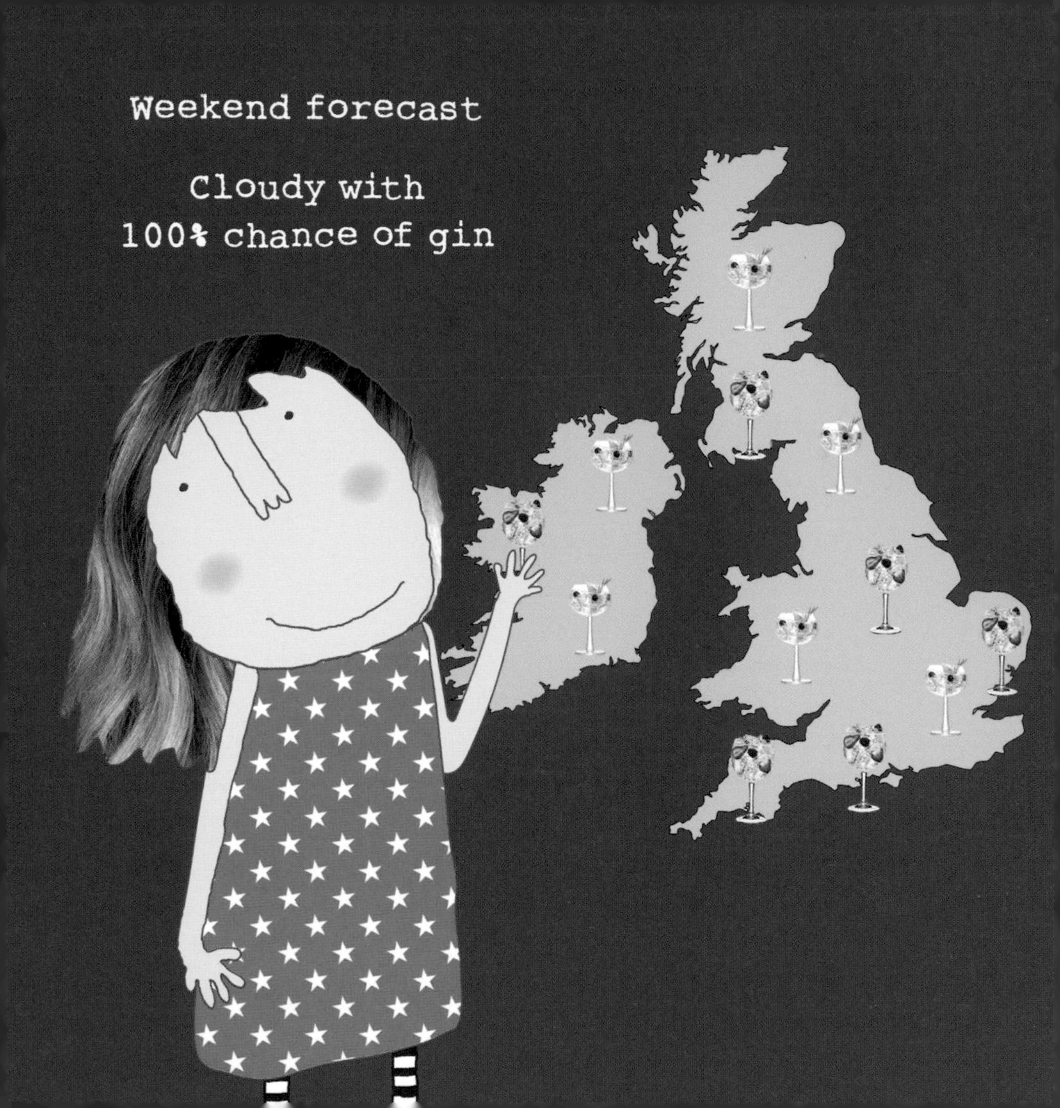
Weekend forecast
Cloudy with
100% chance of gin

Nothing tastes as good as skinny feels

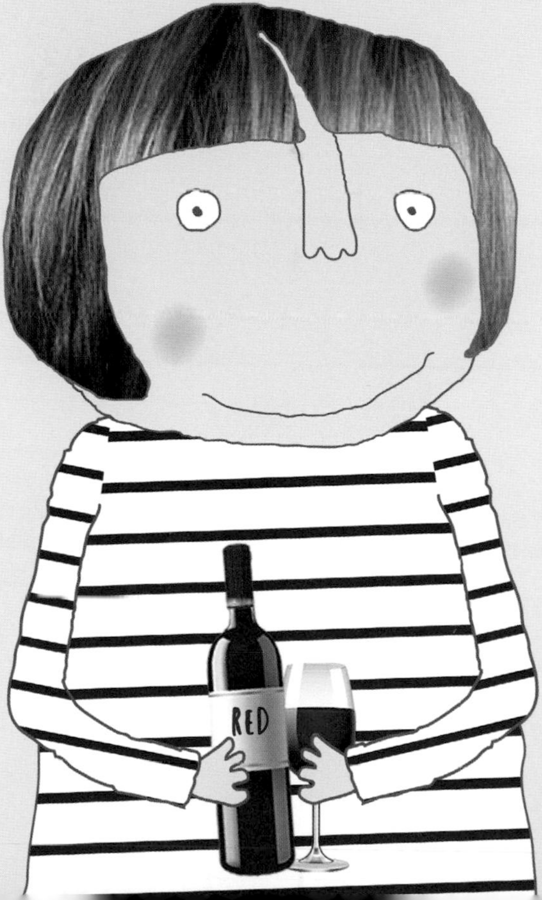
RED

Except wine

Wine tastes
like skinny can
go f**k itself

I'm having five wines

It's called a tasting
and it's classy

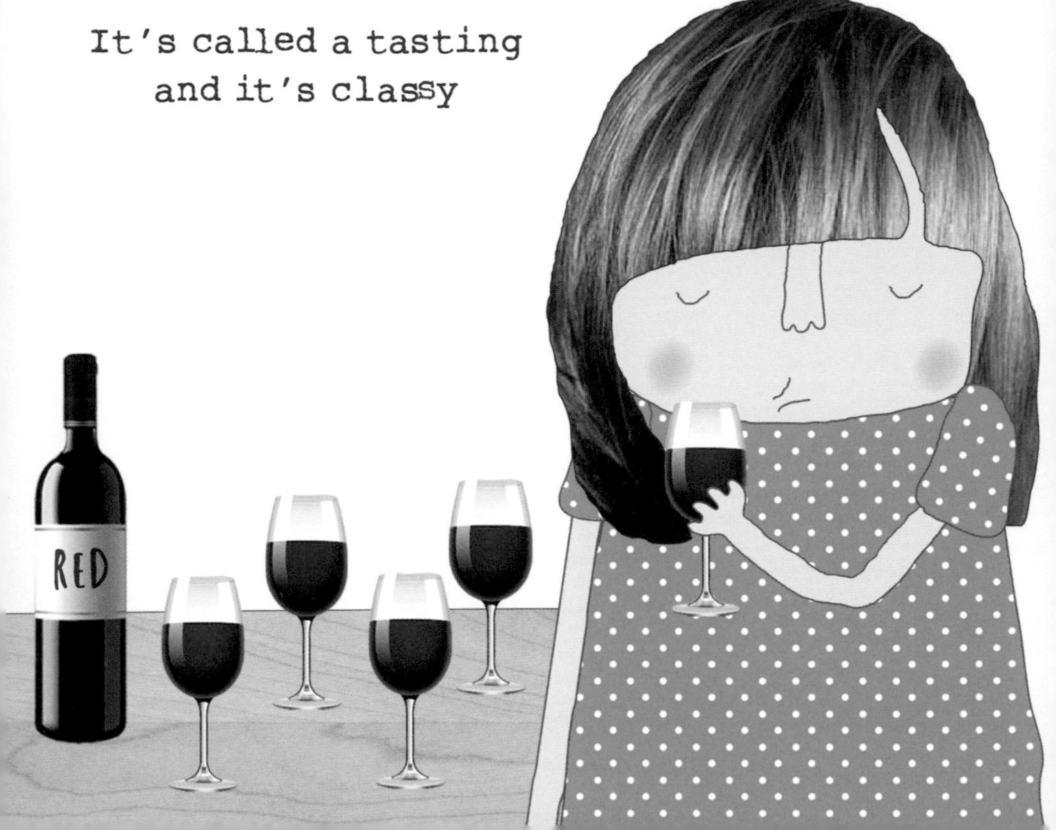
RED

Let's get this party started

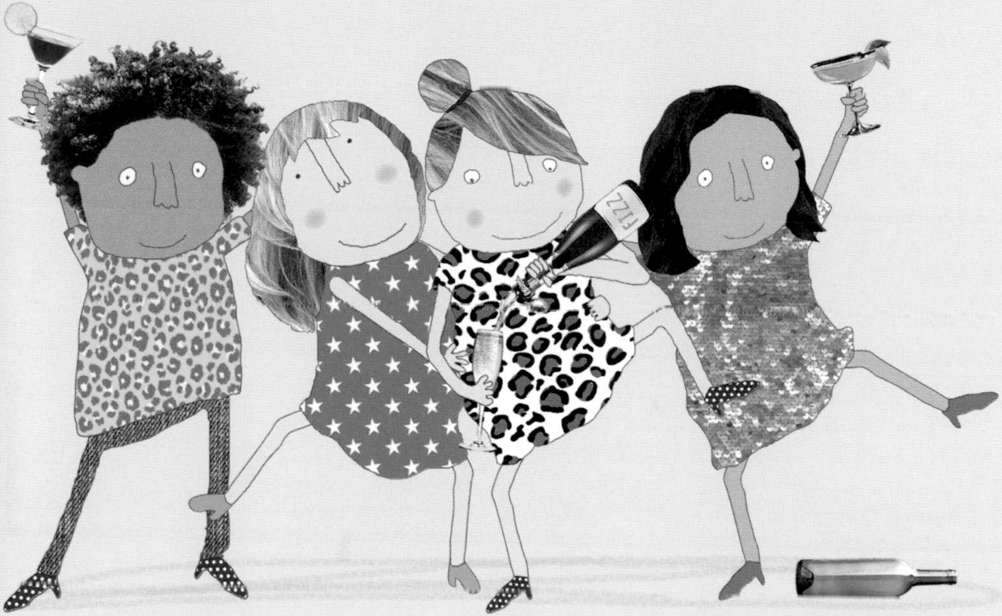
FIZZ

Standards aren't just going
to lower themselves

We're not really adults

We're just tall children who drink wine

All hail!
The Duchess of Fizz

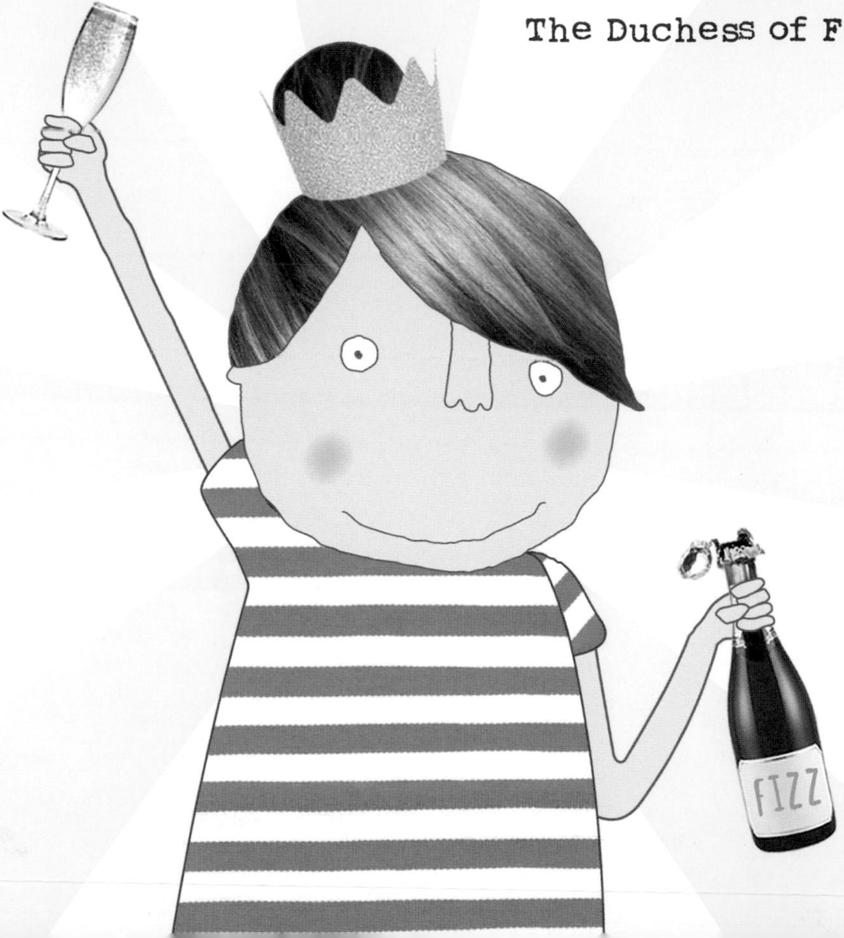
FIZZ

Every day I say to myself,
'Susan, you must give up drinking'

Luckily my name's
not Susan

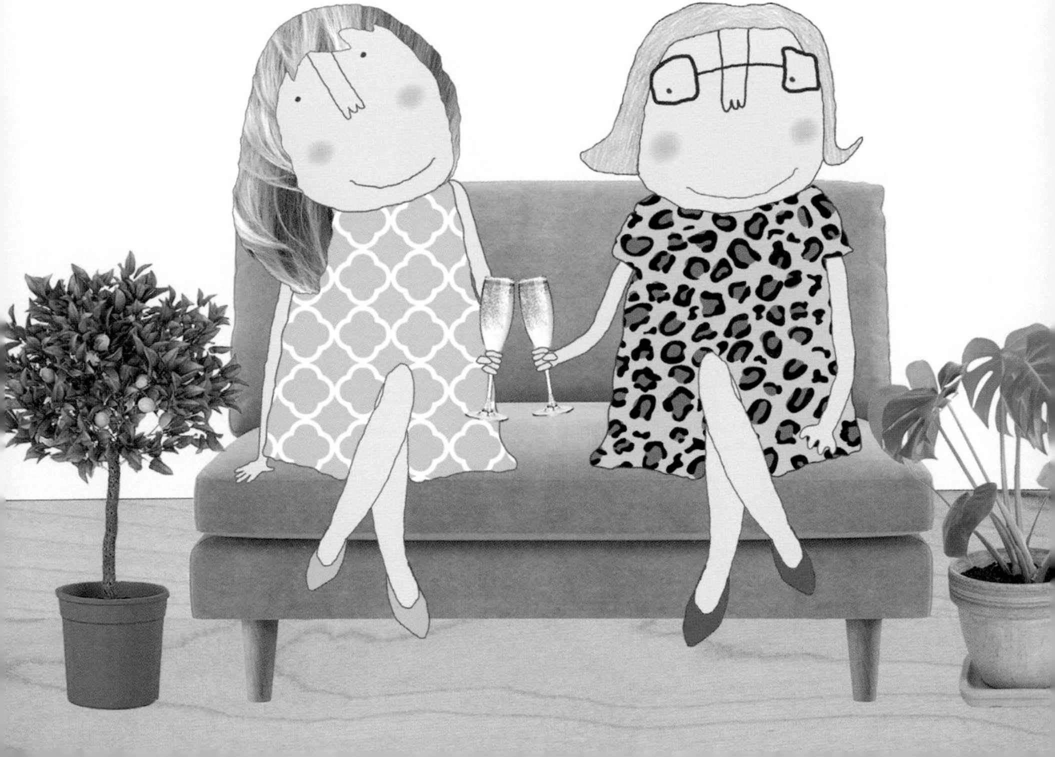

Gin goes in

Fun comes out

I'll come out for one
but I can't get drunk

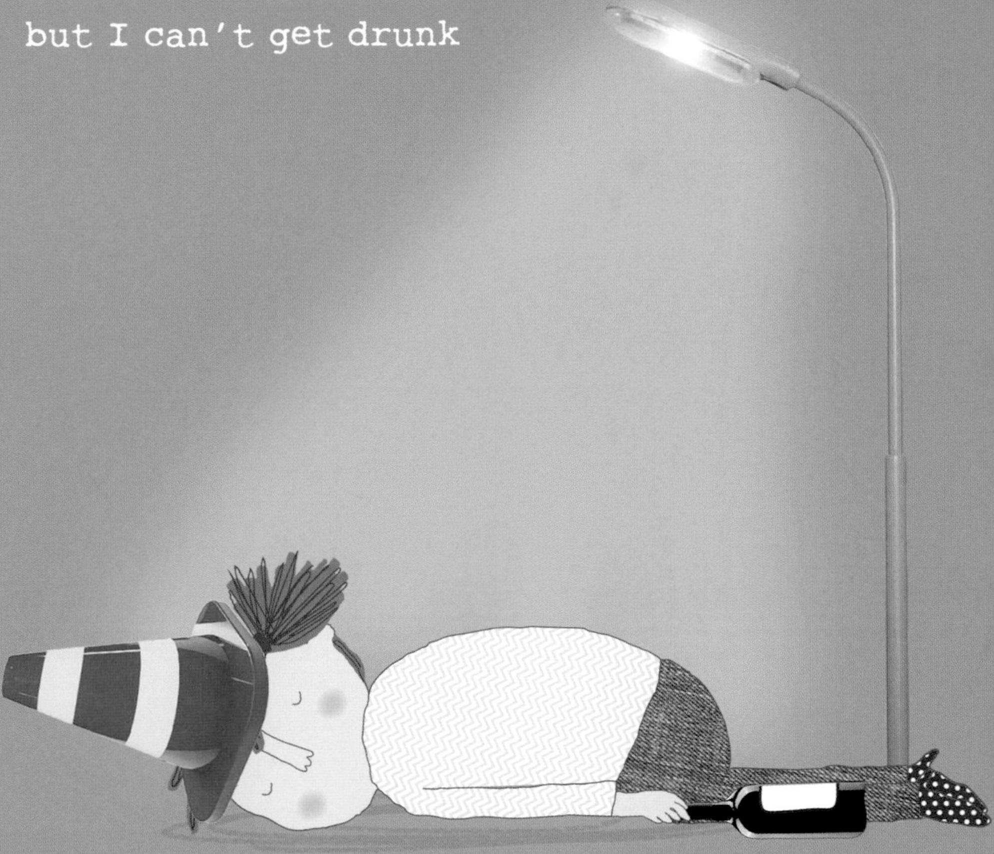

Imagine drinking and not taking it too far every single time and feeling OK the next day

Just imagine

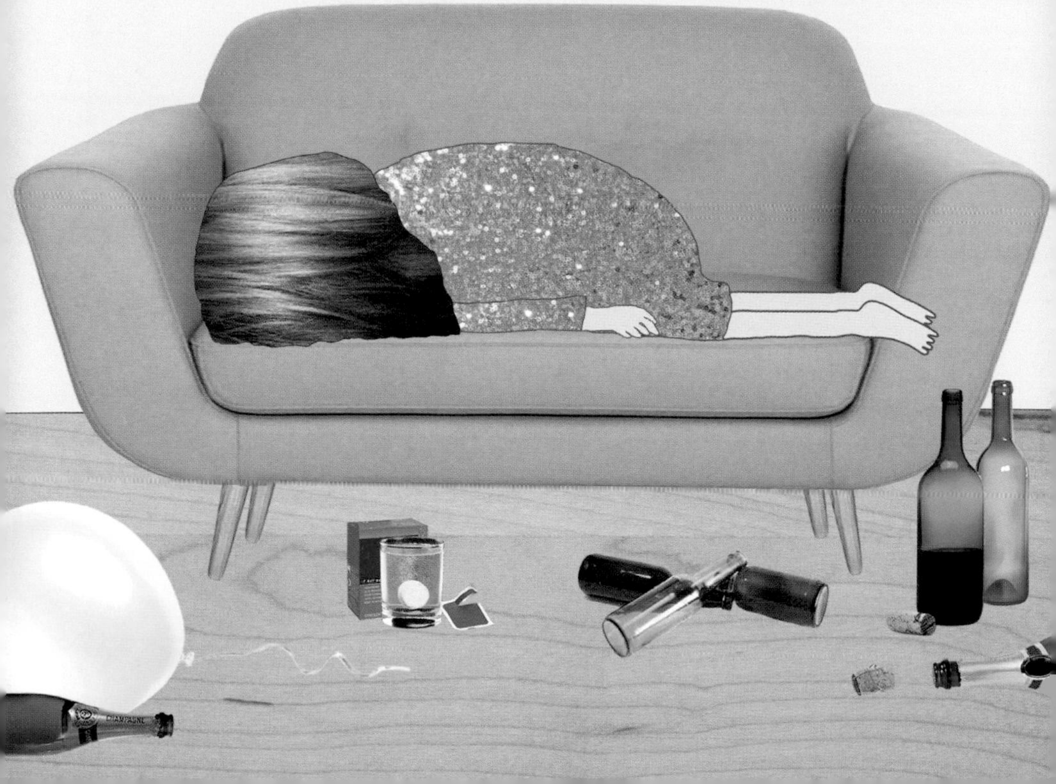

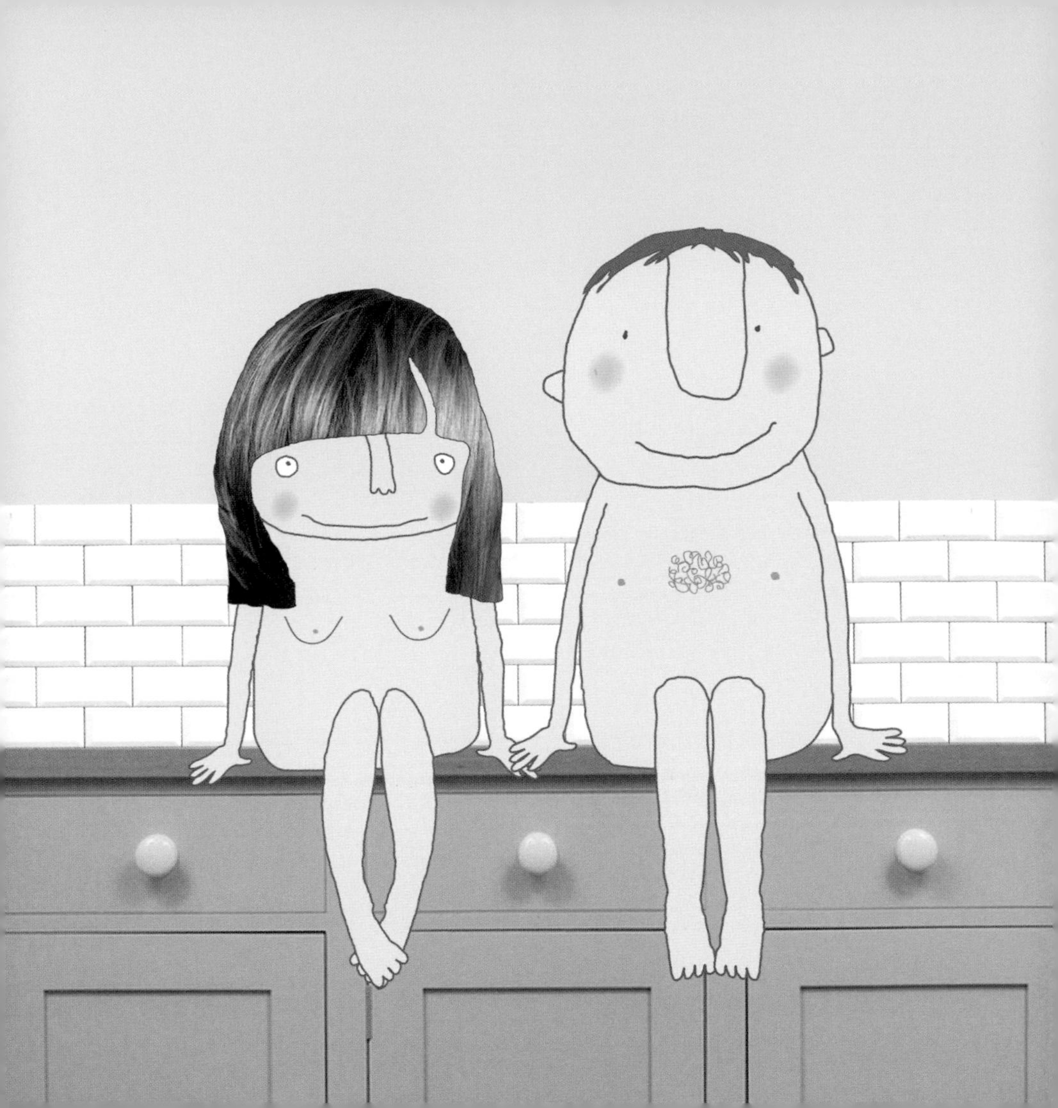

Partners in Crime

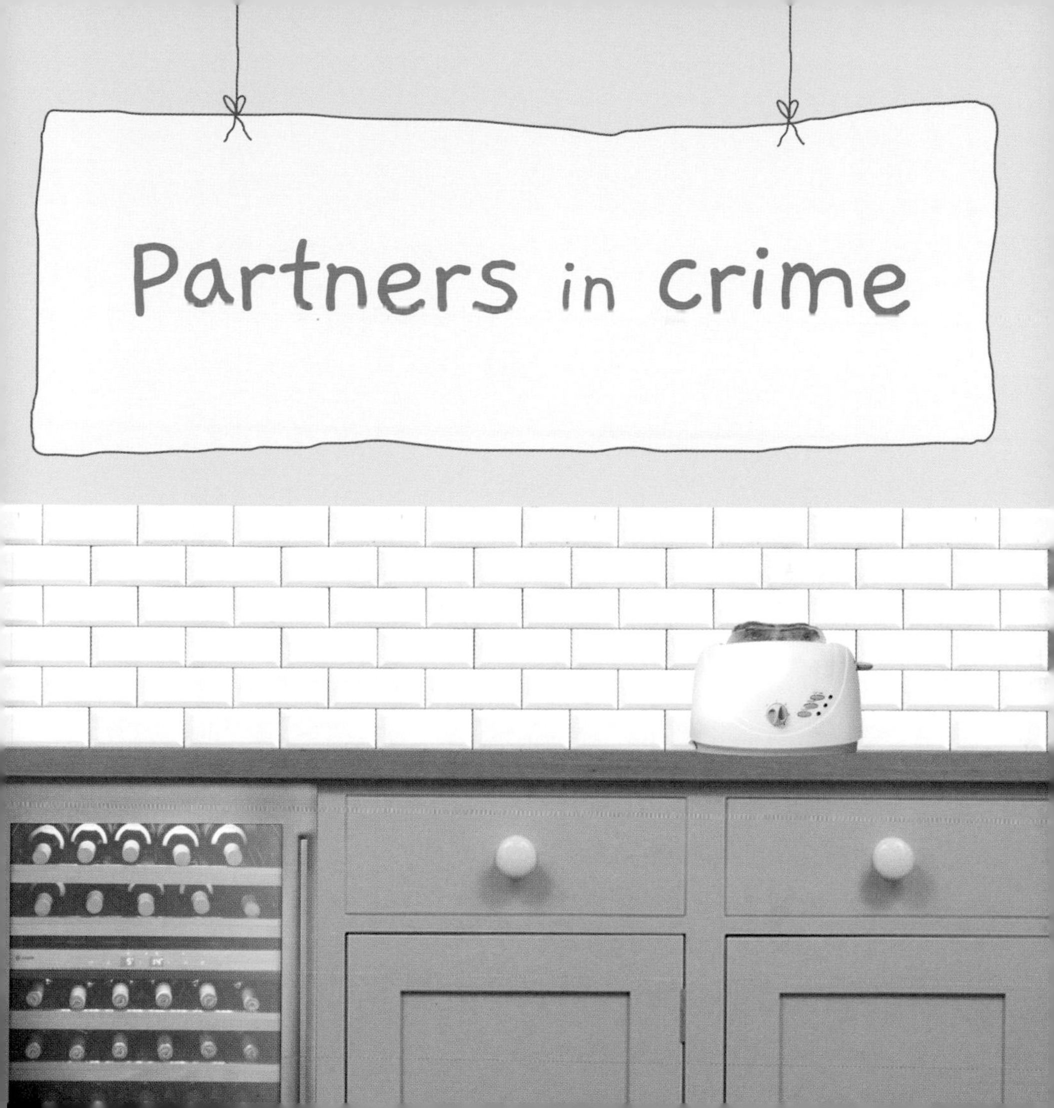

Your soulmate is basically someone you like more than anyone else even though they're still really really annoying

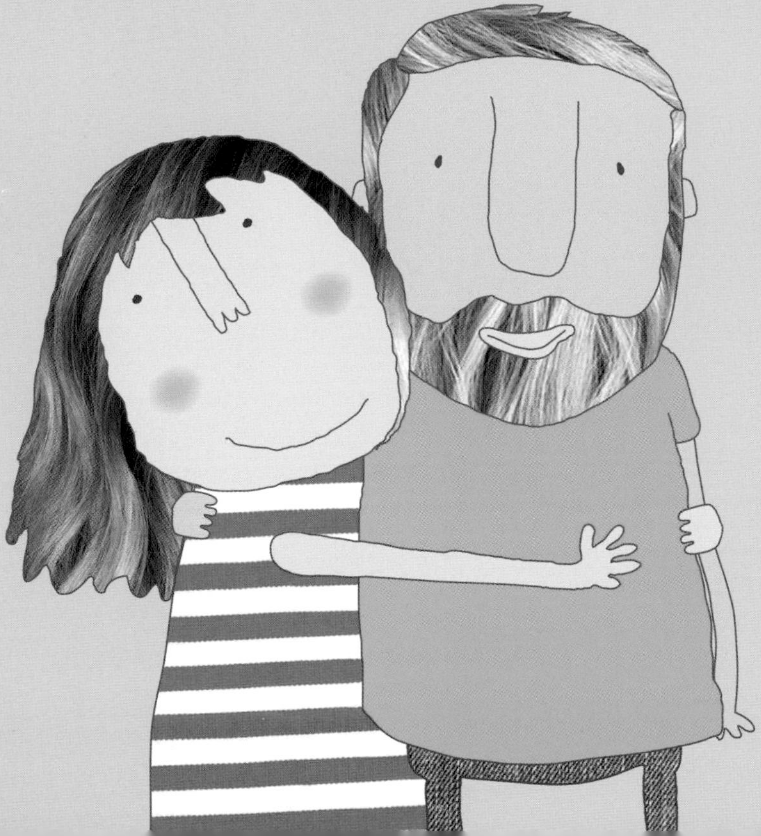

This could be us

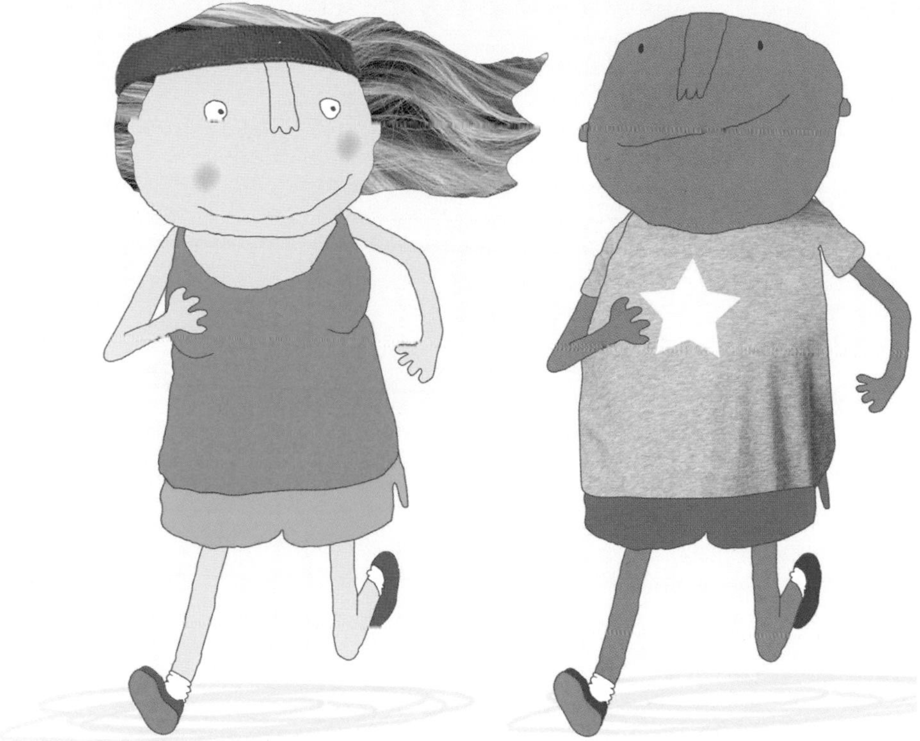

But we like Netflix. Not running.

Being with you is like
winning the lottery but with no money

I married a man
who doesn't like the heating on

so we compromise and have the heating on

Marriage is like having a best friend

who doesn't remember anything you say

He's a knob

but he's **MY** knob

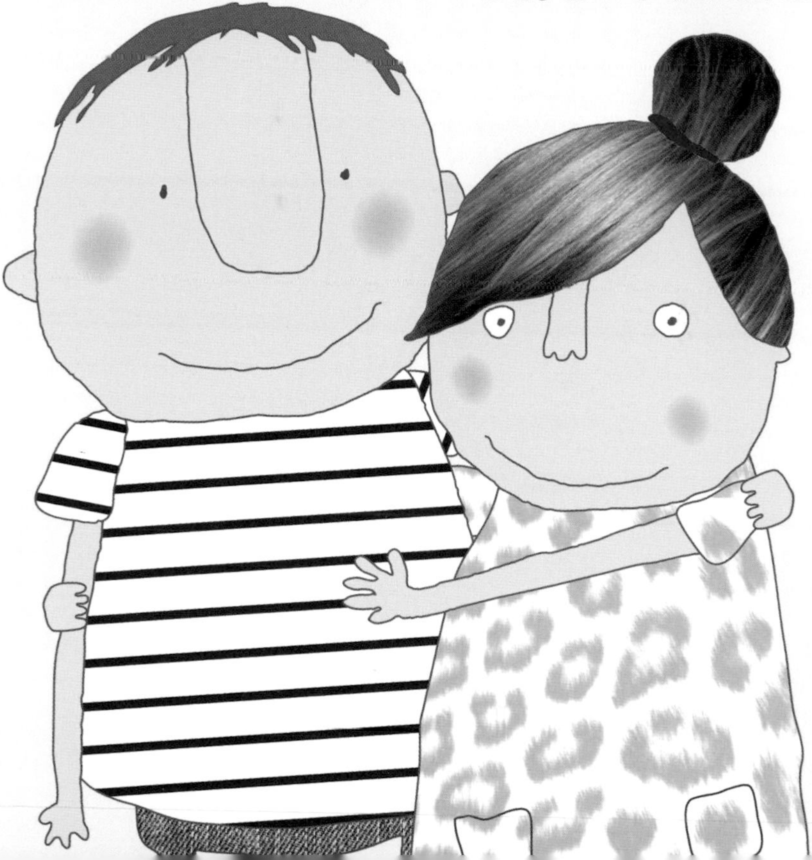

Netflix and too much chill

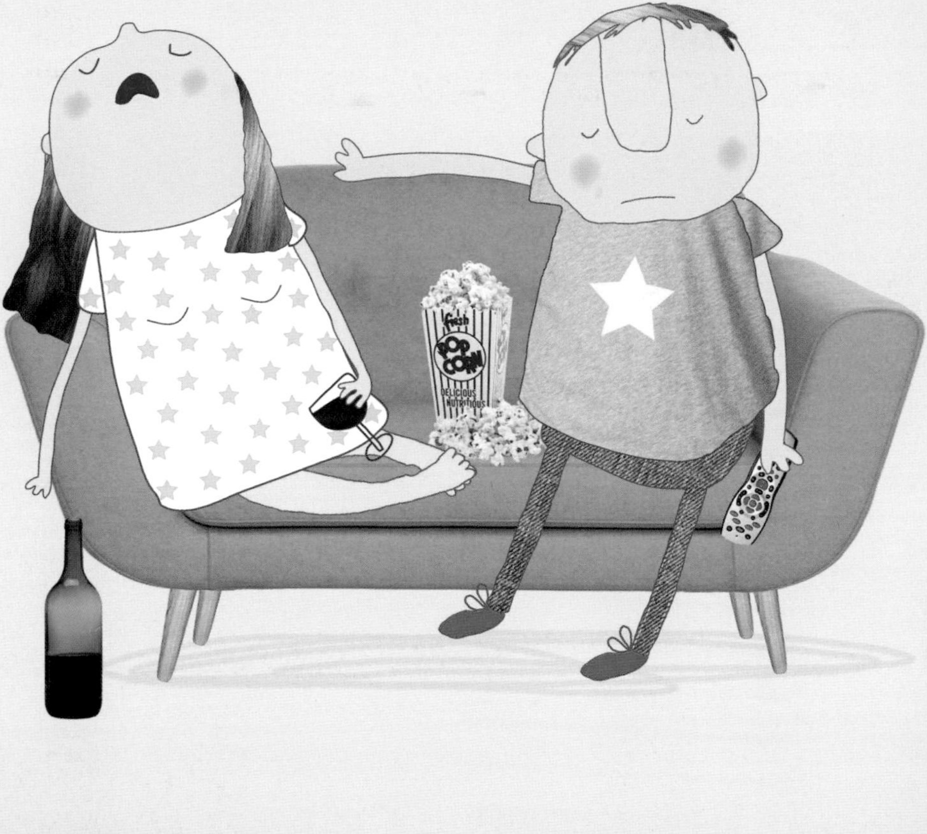
fresh
POP CORN
DELICIOUS
NUTRITIOUS

Their relationship survived IKEA and they lived happily ever after

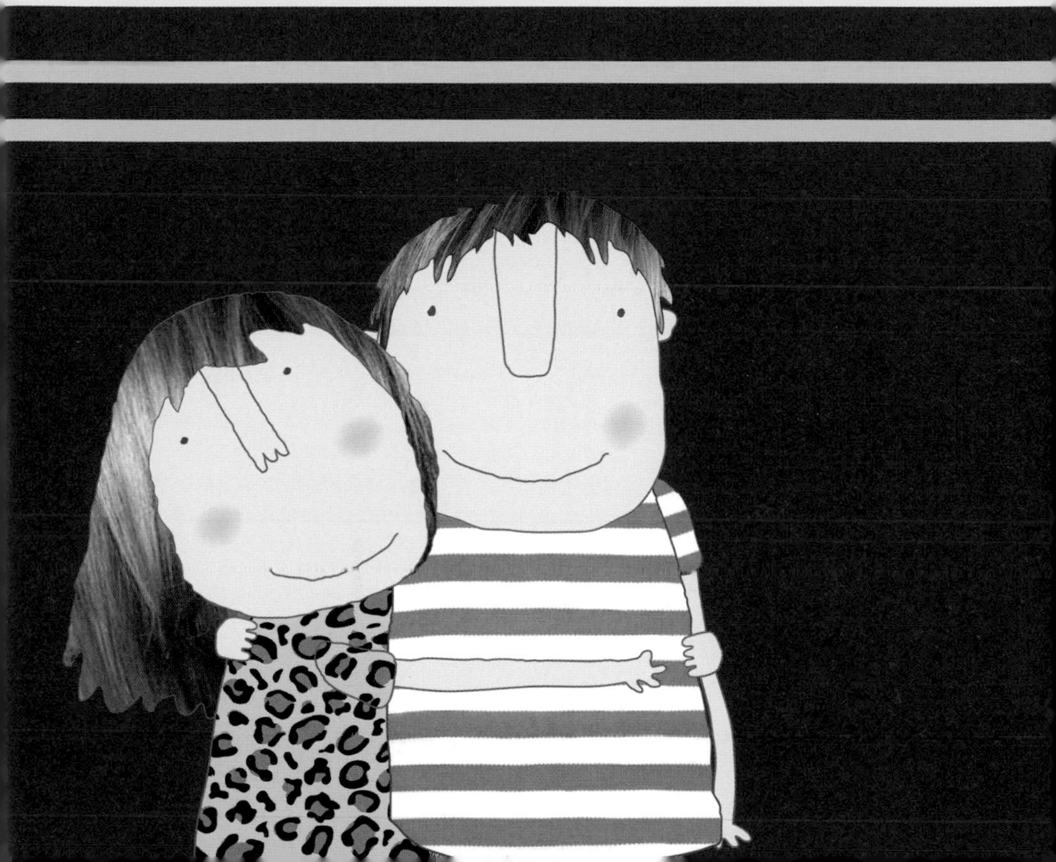

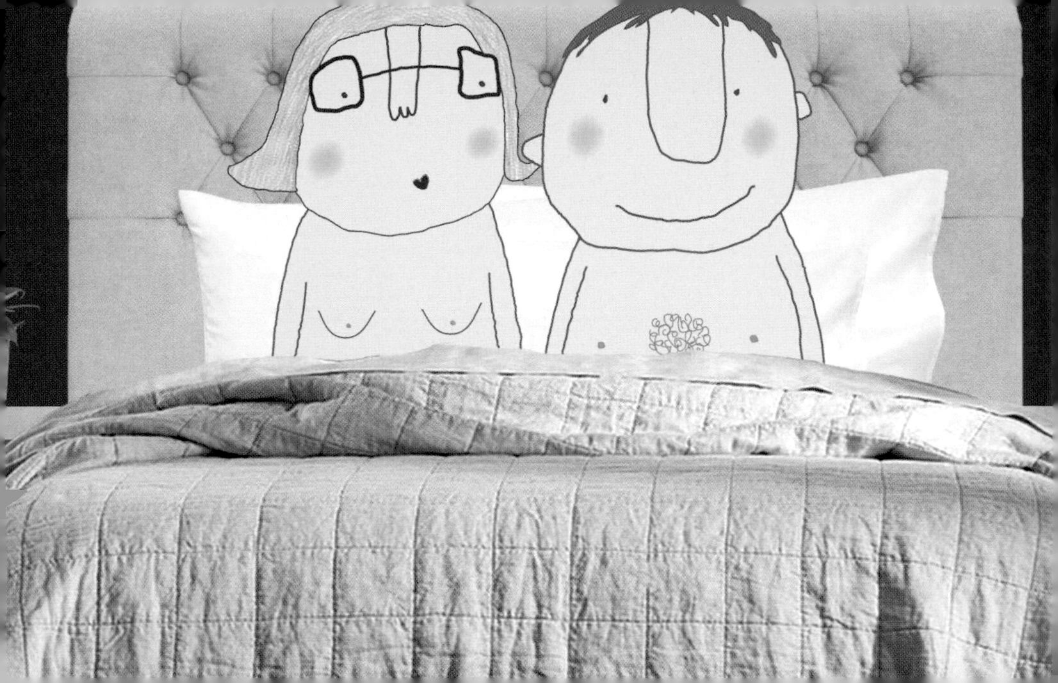

Funny business

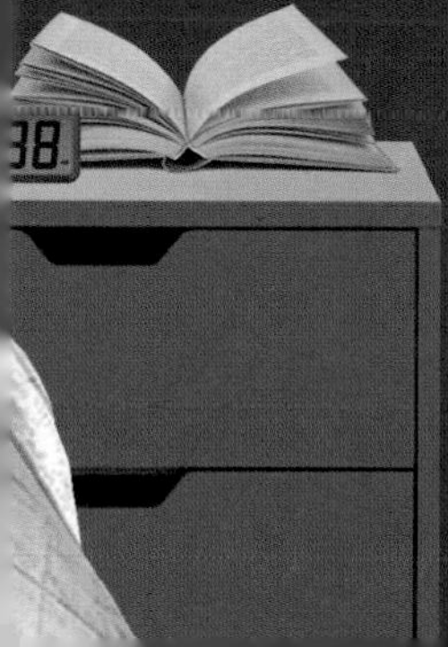

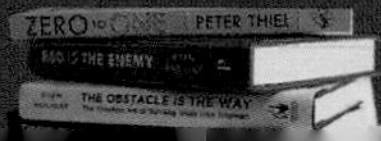
ZERO to ONE PETER THIEL
EGO IS THE ENEMY
THE OBSTACLE IS THE WAY

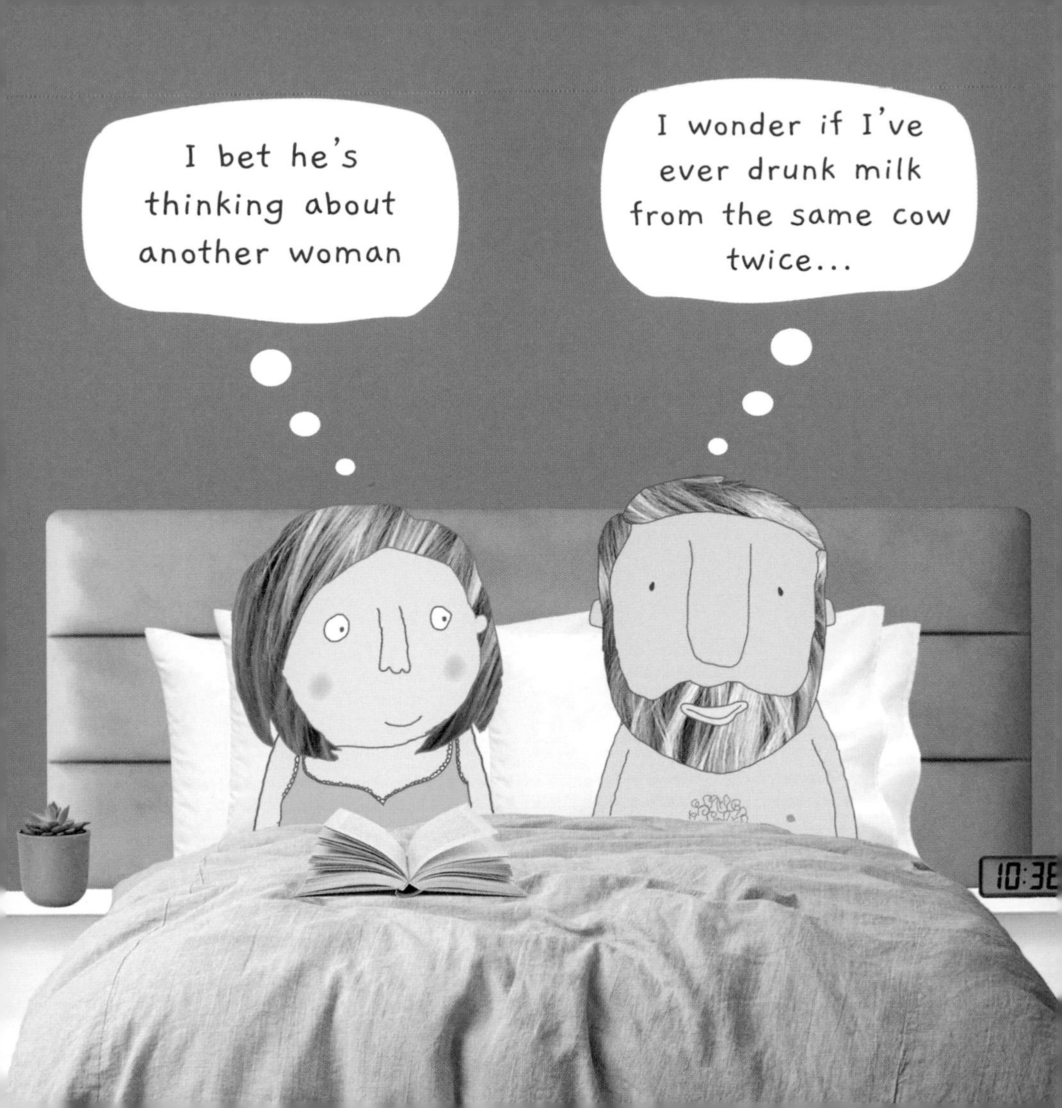
I bet he's thinking about another woman
I wonder if I've ever drunk milk from the same cow twice...
10:38

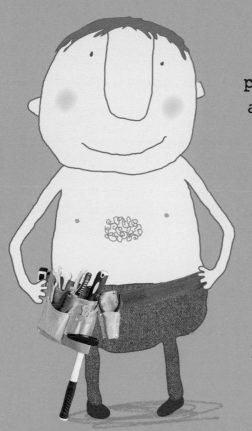

Porn gives young people an unrealistic and unhealthy idea...

...of how quickly a plumber will come to your house

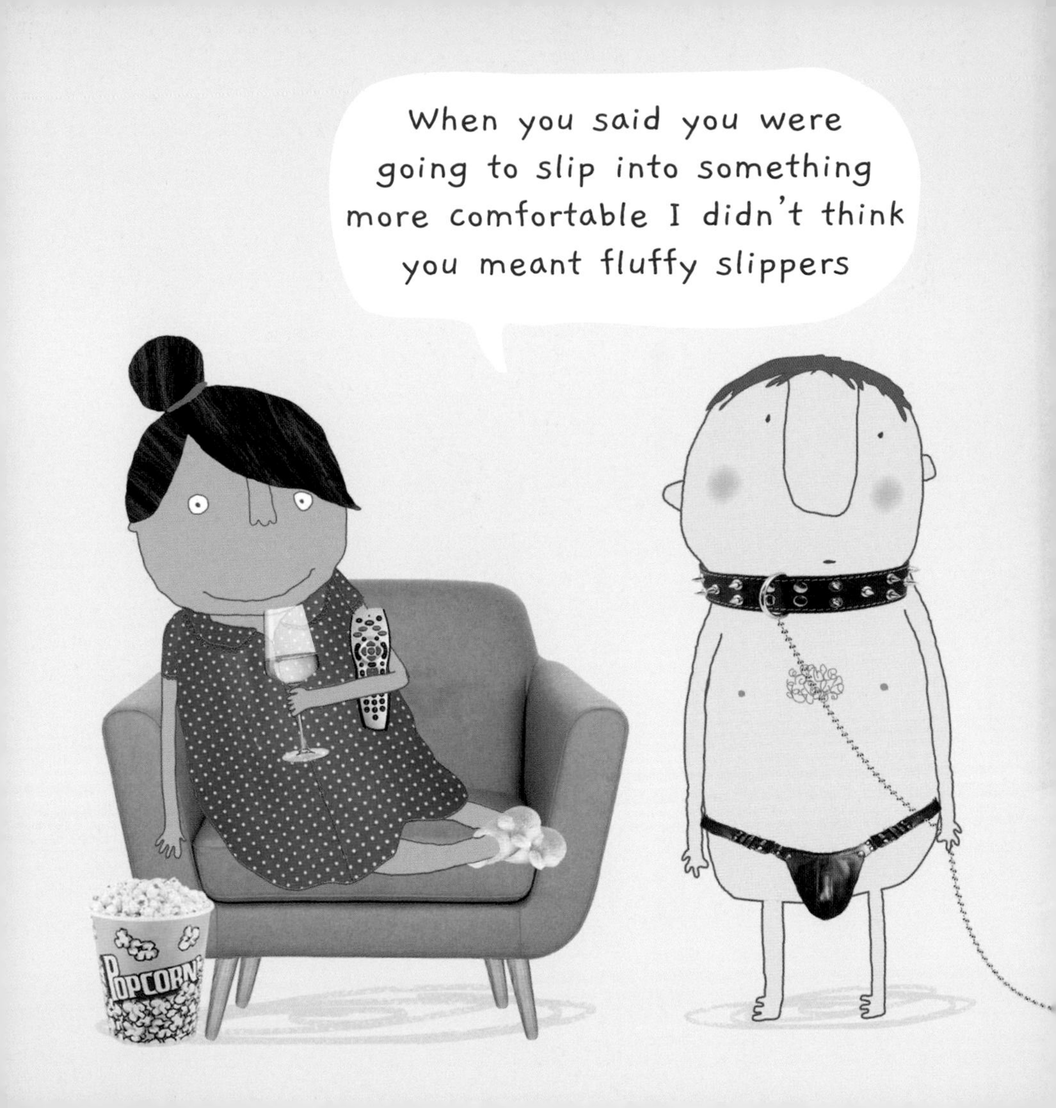
When you said you were going to slip into something more comfortable I didn't think you meant fluffy slippers
POPCORN

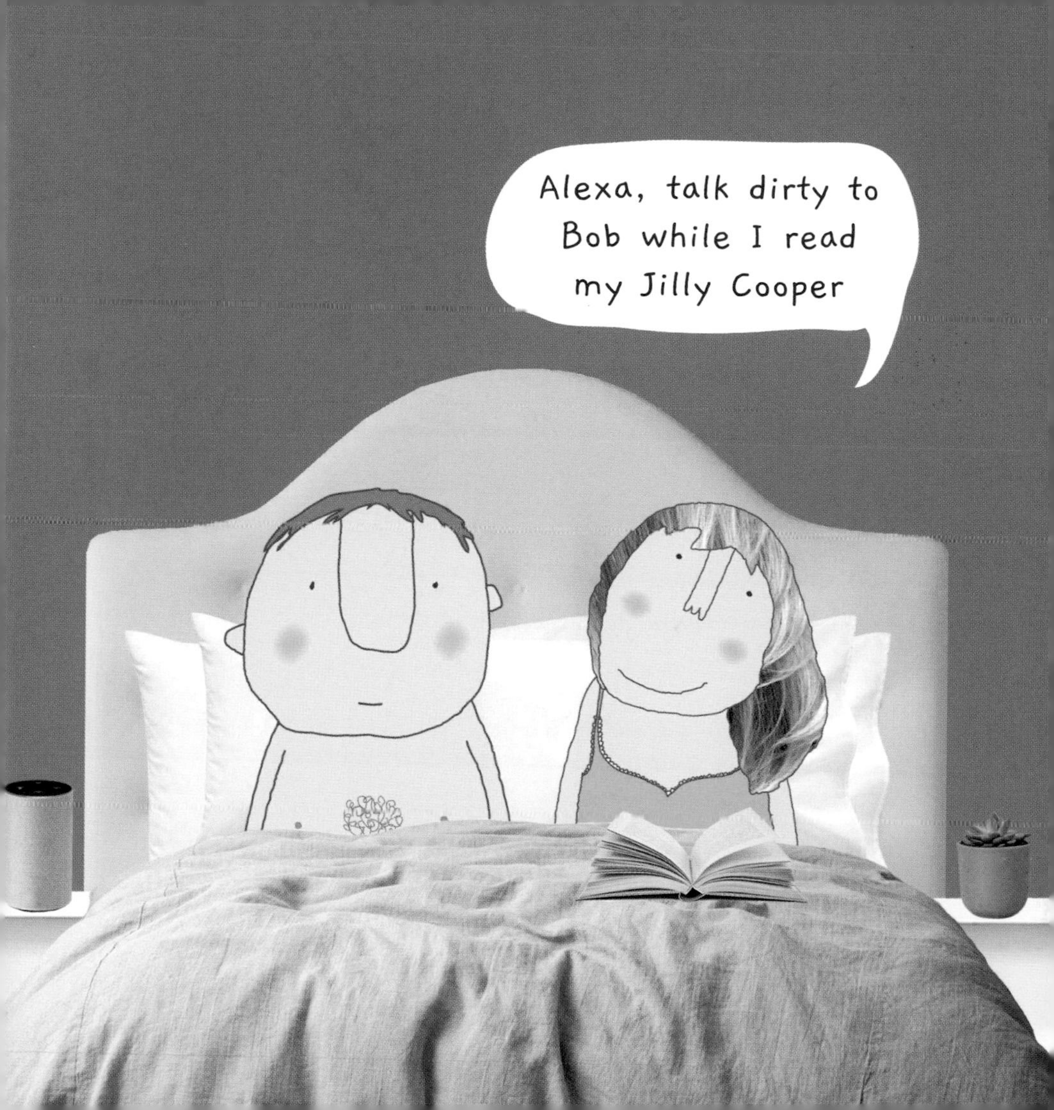
Alexa, talk dirty to Bob while I read my Jilly Cooper

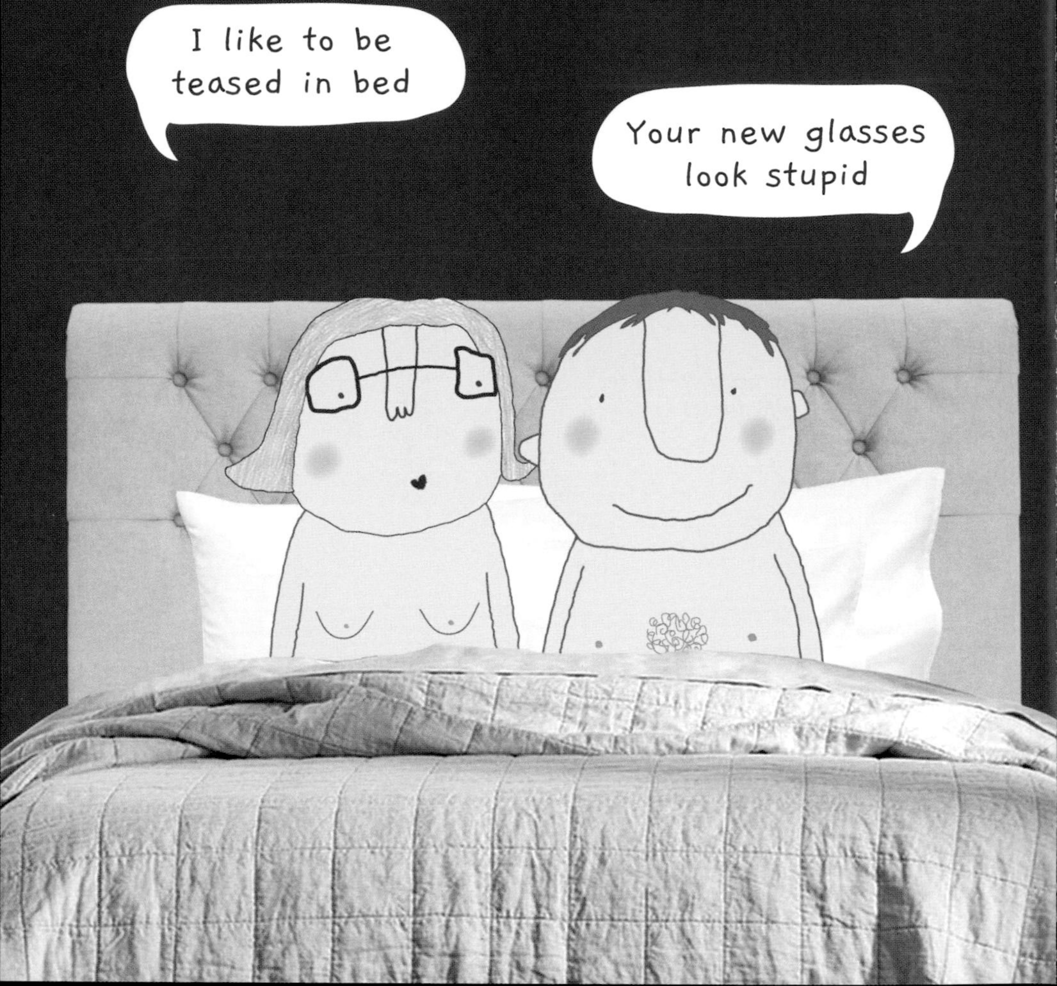
I like to be teased in bed
Your new glasses look stupid

Fifty Shades of Washing Up

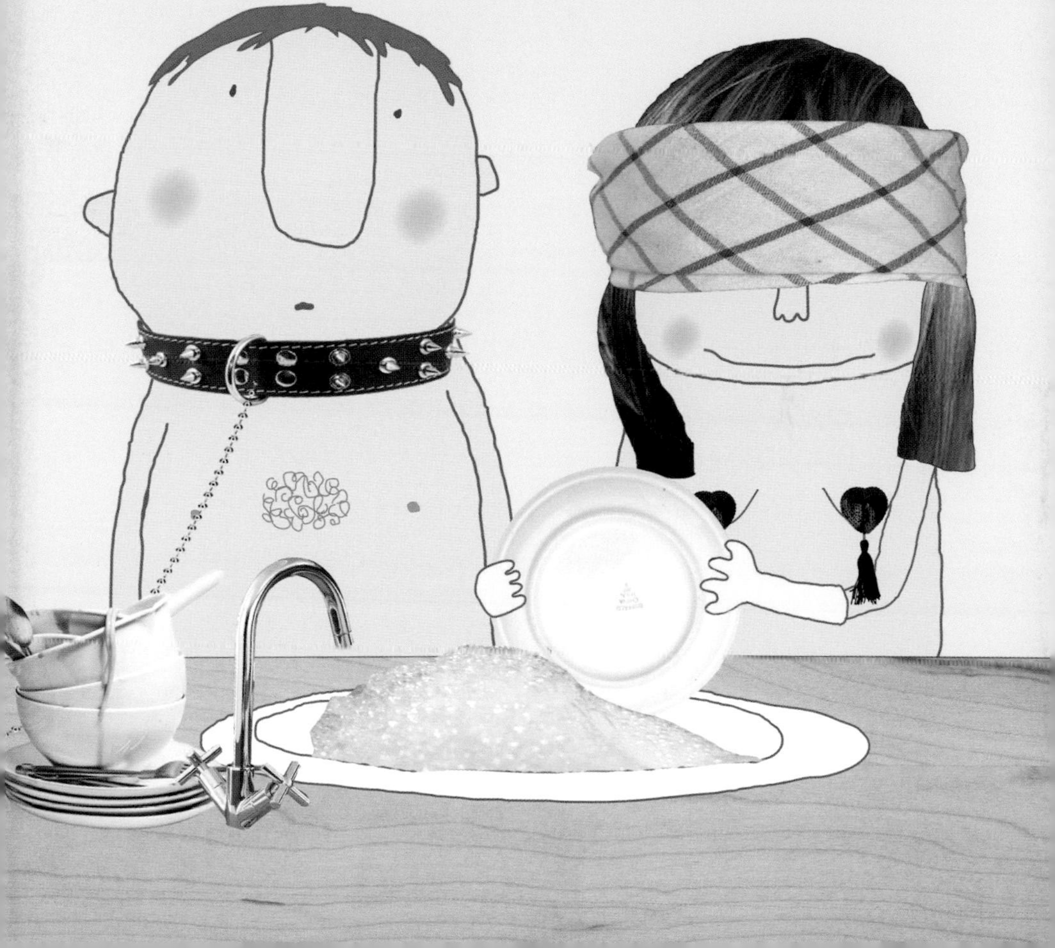

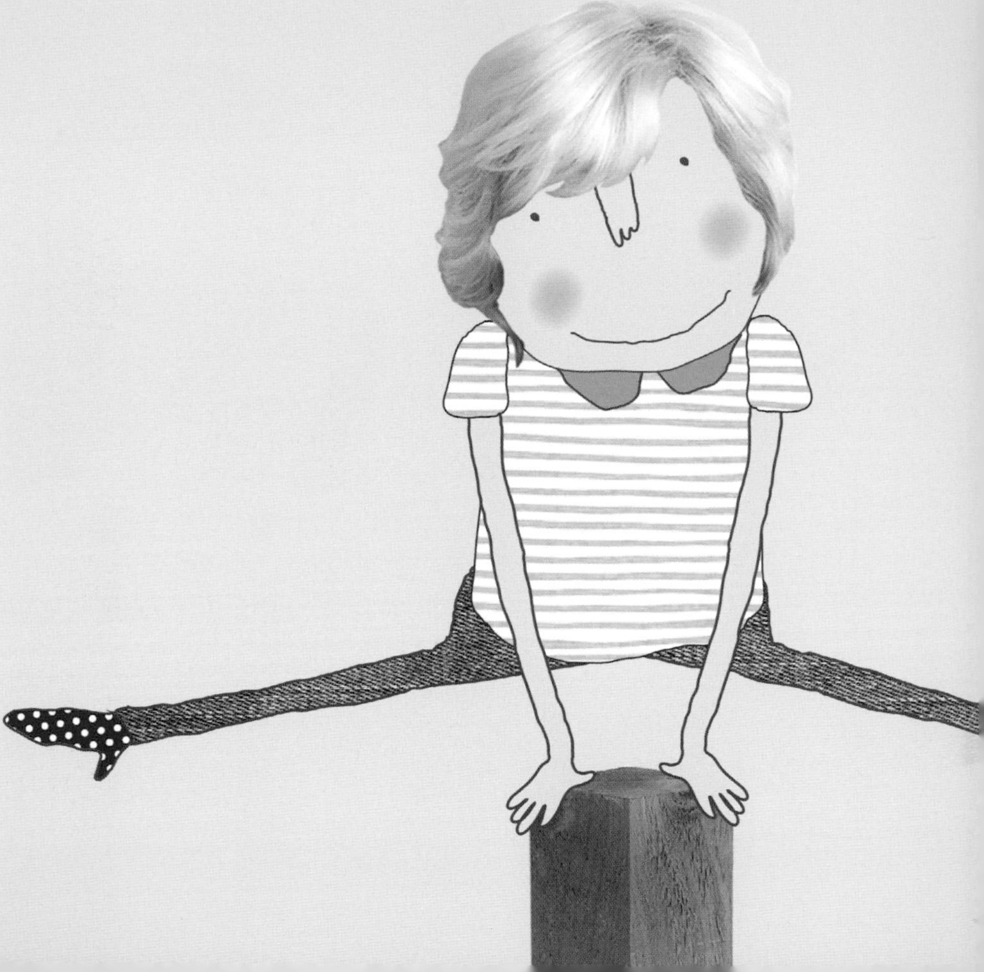

Aging disgracefully

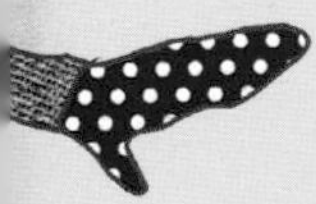

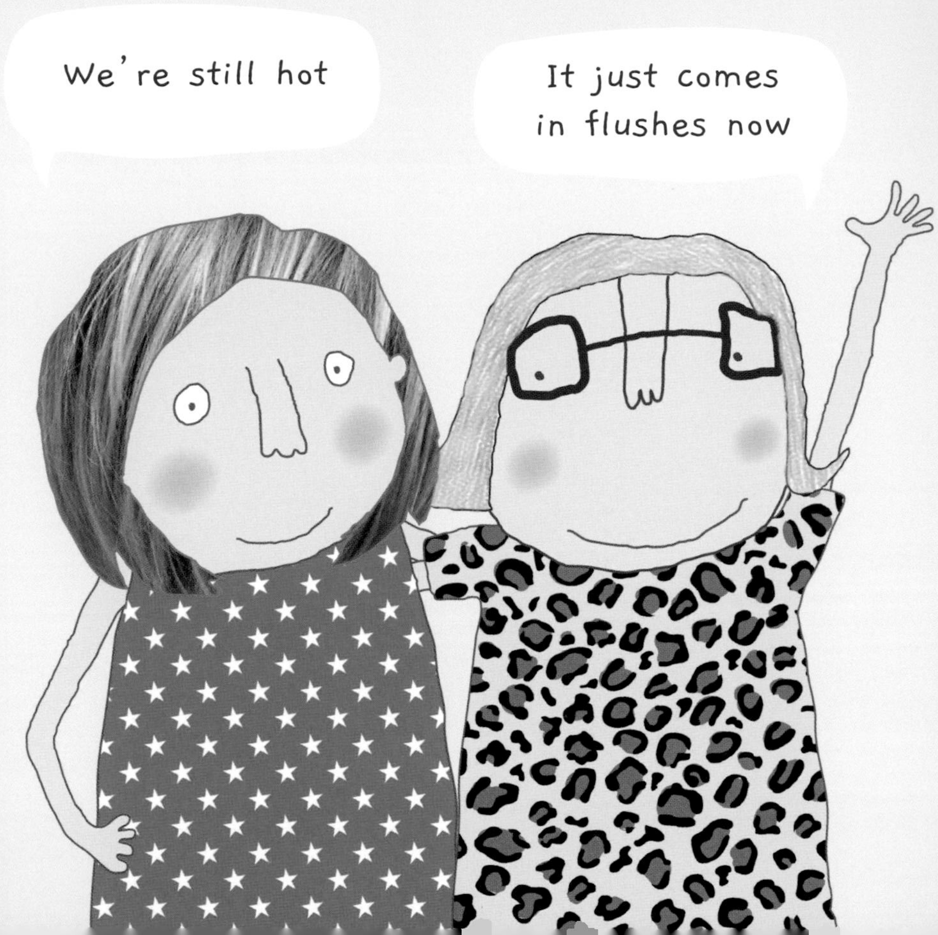
We're still hot
It just comes in flushes now

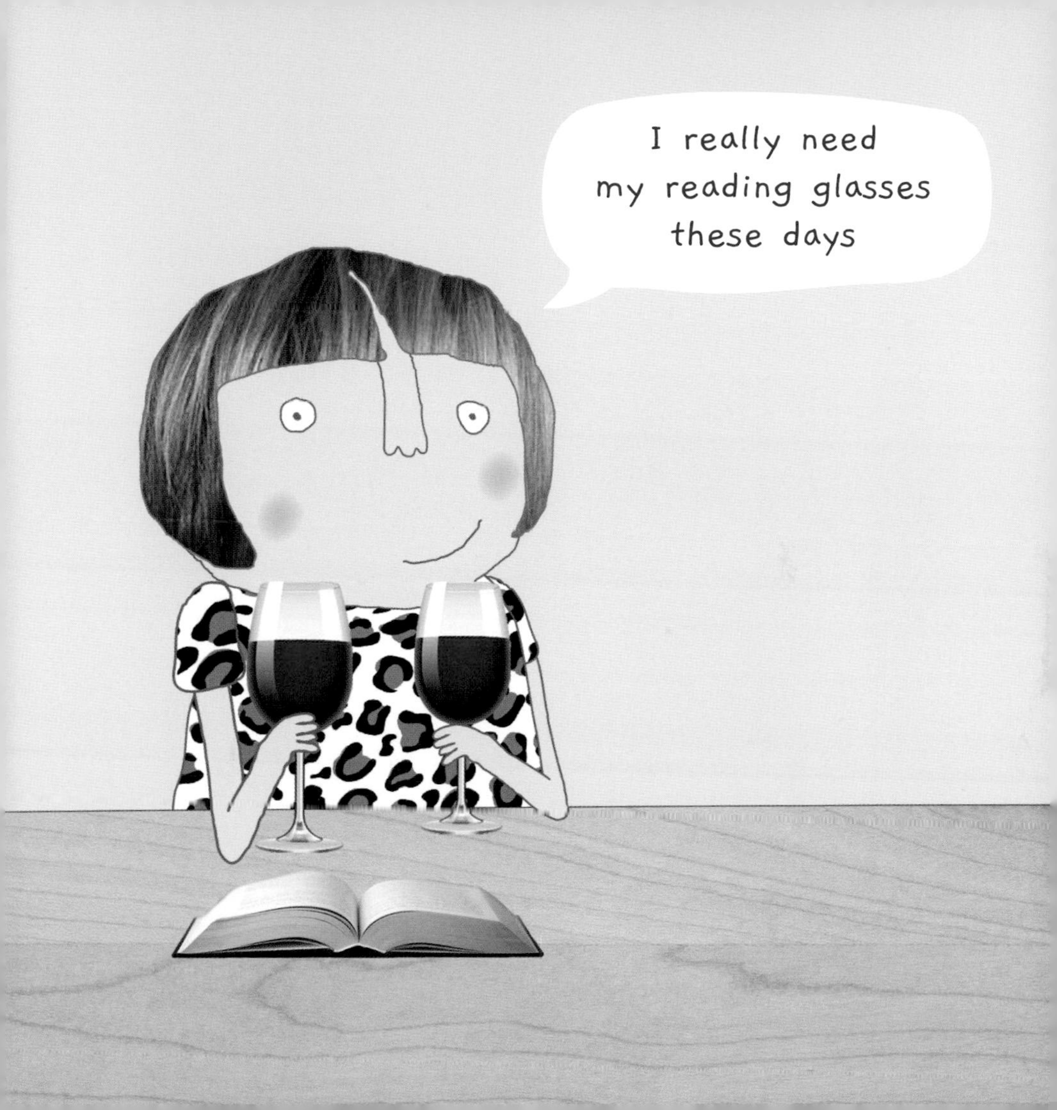
I really need my reading glasses these days

Knitting is
my superpower

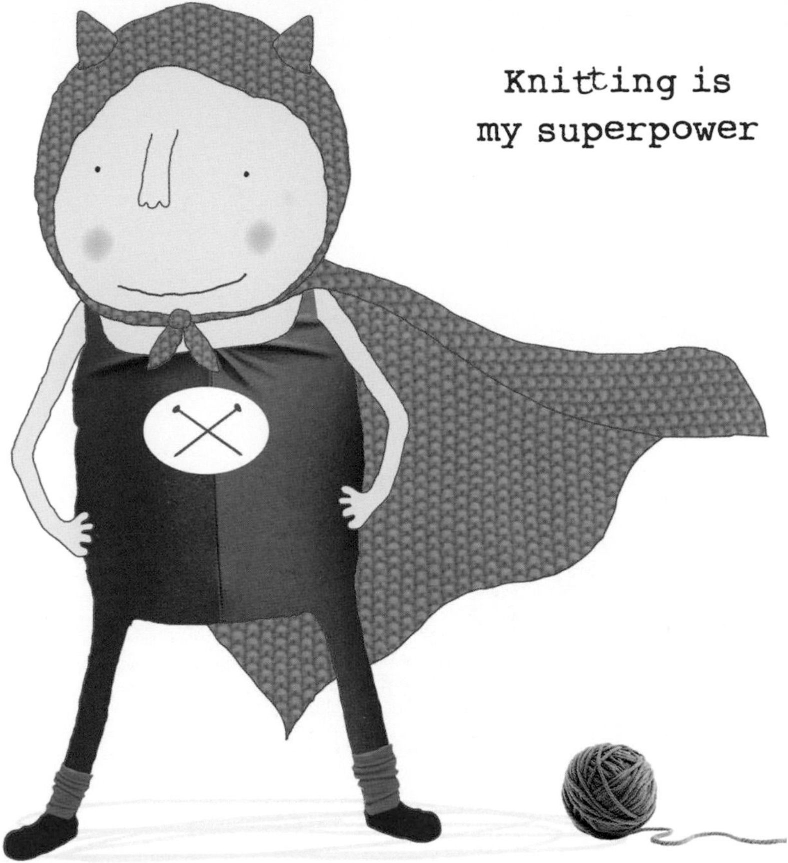

You're never too old to throw on
some leopard print and be bloody fabulous

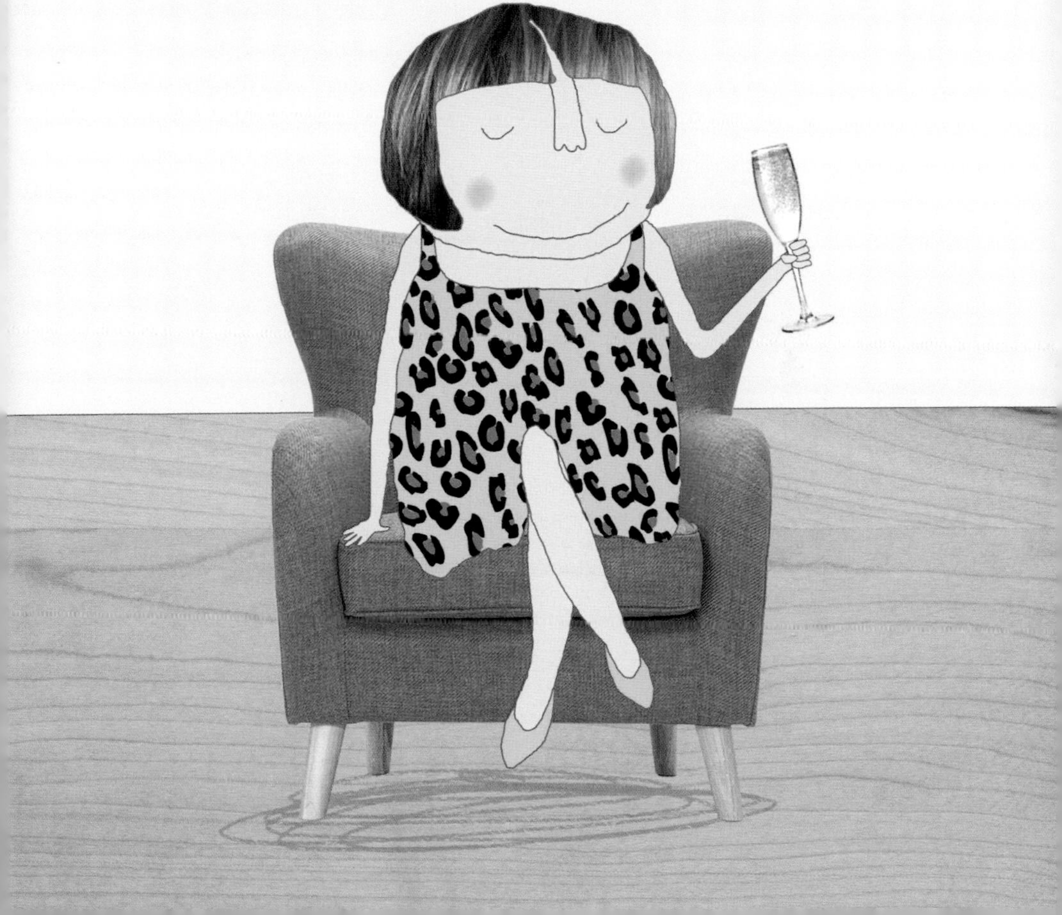

Go braless
It'll pull the wrinkles out of your face

With a body like that, who needs hair?

Goodbye tension

Hello pension

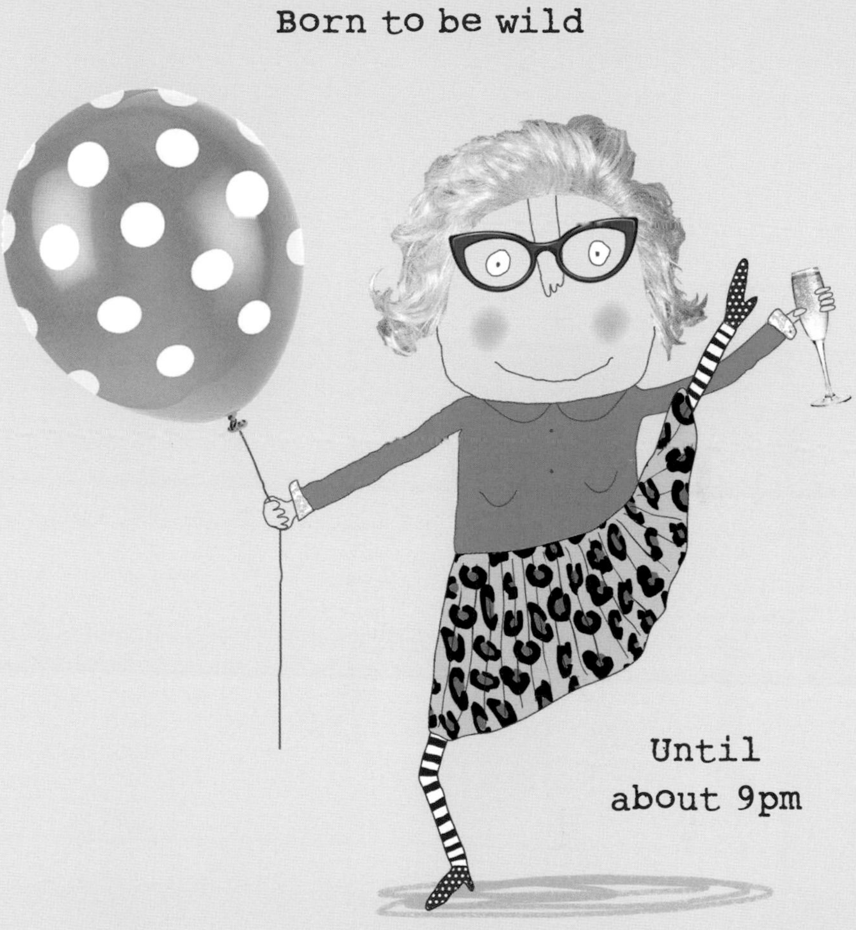
Born to be wild
Until
about 9pm

When you grow up,
people stop asking you
what your favourite
dinosaur is

They don't even care

Let's be friends till we're old

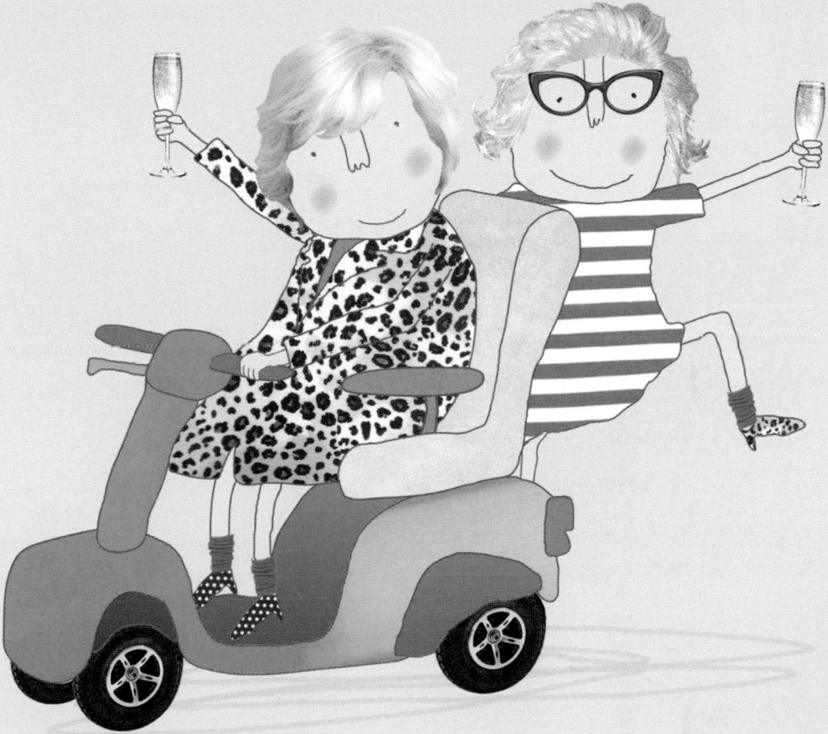

and I can blame the smell of wee on you

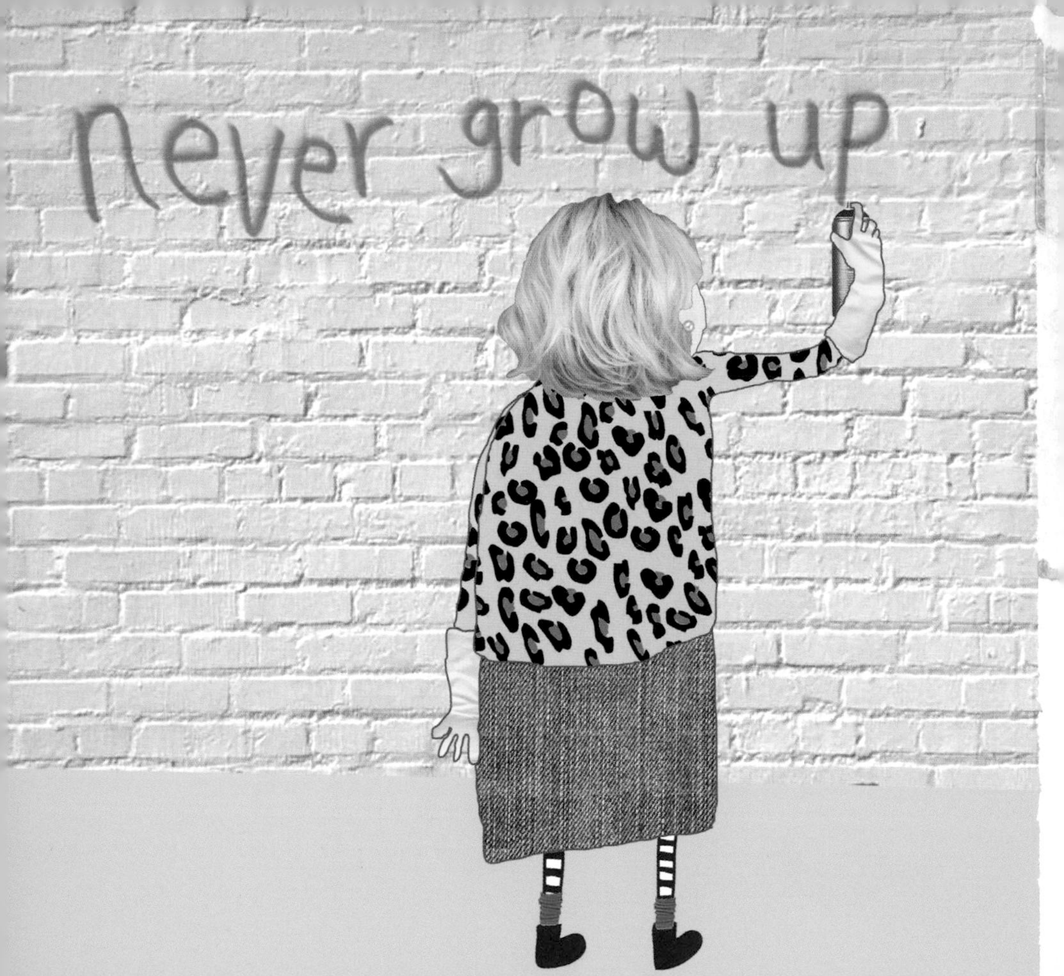
never grow up

It's for old people